Praise for Colin Wee's *Breaking Through: The Secrets of Bassai Dai Kata*

I do not study *Bassai Dai*, but I can see many of its movements within our Ch'ang Hon Taekwon-do *tuls*, or patterns. It is clear that the principles and applications *Sabumnim* Wee shares in *Breaking Through: The Secrets of Bassai Dai Kata* will benefit students of Karate, Tae Kwon Do and other traditional striking arts alike. Highly recommended!

> **Stuart Anslow, 6th Dan, Ch'ang Hon Taekwon-Do**
> Owner & Instructor at Rayners Lane Taekwon-do Academy
> Editor of *Totally Tae Kwon Do* magazine
> Author of *From Creation to Unification: The Complete Histories Behind the Ch'ang Hon (ITF) Patterns*, and five additional books about the Ch'ang Hon (ITF) patterns and applications
> HarrowTKD.com, TotallyTKD.com

When I was asked to review Colin Wee's book *Breaking Through: The Secrets of Bassai Dai Kata*, I was hesitant. It is, after all, a *bunkai*-book. Often *bunkai*—or *kata*-interpretation—are desperate attempts to legitimize the time spent on martial art forms when it is obvious that the forms do not reflect actual combat and the *bunkai* are often impractical. However, I quickly realized that this book is not about *Bassai Dai Kata*. It is rather one martial art school's journey of self-discovery. While the book does contain *bunkai*, the various applications in the book are not the goal; instead of trying to conform to the *kata* in ways that are contrived, the *kata*-movements are seen more as springboards from where to explore techniques, resulting in what Dan Djurdjevic, a talented martial artist and blogger, calls "dynamic context drills." What I would criticize as forced applications in other *bunkai*-books is the very point of Wee's book: creative and playful exploration that does not try to imitate the *kata* in unnatural and unrealistic ways. Rather, Wee offers strategic principles, illustrated through "applications" from *Bassai Dai Kata*. *Breaking Through*'s real contribution to martial arts literature is not that it offers applications from *Bassai Dai Kata* but instead inspires the reader to be more cognitive about their own martial arts practice and inspires every practitioner to be more experimental with their own martial arts tradition.

> **Dr Sanko Lewis, 5th Dan, ITF Taekwon-Do**
> Martial Arts Researcher, South Korea
> SankoLewis.com

What makes a good teacher? It is the ability to change the way people look at their chosen area of study, bring it to life and provide students with tools to make their own way. That is what I see in *Colin Wee's Breaking Through: The Secrets of Bassai Dai Kata*. Colin has developed a methodology that can be applied to this *kata*, to other forms or to other endeavours beyond martial arts. I am thoroughly impressed.

> **Simon O'Neill, 4th Dan**
> Author of *The Taegeuk Cipher* and its companion video series
> PalKwon.com

Colin Wee has written a book I would recommend for every martial artist regardless of style. It is a timely reminder that the martial arts by its collective nature embodies culture and tradition, as well as ongoing empirical research and refinement. Each chapter concisely describes and dissects movement and application but, more importantly, goes beyond literal translation and emphasizes analysis and extrapolation for effective improvement. Not just for *Bassai kata* but for all traditional forms or patterns. The inclusion of reflective questions at the end of each chapter neatly completes the three types of reflective practice necessary for continuous improvement. I have no doubt that any practitioner who absorbs the lessons from *Breaking Through: The Secrets of Bassai Dai Kata* will be reflecting on their own style through a different lens forged from the insight and knowledge gained from its pages.

Dr. Prakash Menon, 2nd Degree Brown Belt, Northern Shaolin *Cheun Fa*
Singapore

In a world where so many rush to criticize and divide, Master Wee stands tall as a leader who seeks to celebrate and connect. In *Breaking Through*, Master Wee builds a bridge of respect and value between the traditional and modern, external and internal, and hard and soft. I recommend that all students and teachers of the martial arts follow Master Wee's example of exploring the "Middle Way" as his methodology clearly results in a high degree of both skill and wisdom.

Ando Mierzwa, 8th Degree, Kung Fu San Soo
Owner & Instructor at Happy Life Martial Arts
Founder of *Fight for a Happy Life* martial arts podcast
SenseiAndo.com

I have always thought that Colin Wee is unique in his approach to martial art research. This book also highlights that he's an outstanding communicator. He does a wonderful job dissecting a classical Karate form, or *kata*, transcending technique to enter the realm of concept. If you thought that *kata* is something fixed, incompatible with the ever-changing and unpredictable nature of combat, be ready for a big surprise! Colin's work in *Breaking Through* is an innovative and deep contribution to martial art forms interpretation.

Manuel Adrogué, 8th Dan, ITF-style Taekwon-Do
Chief Instructor at Mudo Jongshin Taekwon-Do Won, Argentina
Taekwon.com.ar

Colin Wee

BREAKING THROUGH

The Secrets of Bassai Dai Kata

Contents copyright © 2023 by **Colin Wee**
Layout copyright © 2023 by Mike Swope.
All rights reserved.

No part of this publication may be reproduced, distributed, or transmitted in any form or by any means, including photocopying, recording, or other electronic or mechanical methods, without the prior written permission of the respective copyright owner, except in the case of brief quotations embodied in critical reviews and certain other noncommercial uses permitted by copyright law. For permission requests, contact the publisher.

Special discounts are available on quantity purchases by corporations, associations, and others. For details, please contact the publisher.

ISBN 978-0-9962640-5-1
First Edition

Special thanks for the following, who provided photographs and other media for this book:

Grandmaster Keith Yates (Pages 2 & 3)
Duncan Yong @dky_photography (Pages 4 & 18)
Thao Le Hoang via Unsplash.com (Page 9)
Sandy Lim (Page 20)
Stuart Anslow & **Mike Swope** (Pages 122–146)

Notice of Liability
The information in this book is distributed without warranty and is only presented as a means of preserving the techniques and principles of Master Colin Wee and Joong Do Kwan. All the information and techniques herein are to be used at the reader's sole discretion. While every precaution has been taken in preparation of this book, neither the author nor publisher shall have any liability to any person or entity with respect to injury, loss or damage caused or alleged to be caused directly or indirectly by the contents of this book or by the procedures or processes described herein. There is no guarantee that the techniques described or shown in this book will be safe or effective in any self-defense situation or otherwise. You may be injured if you apply or train the techniques in this book. Consult a physician regarding whether to attempt any technique described in this book. Specific self-defense responses illustrated in this book may not be justified in any particular situation in view of circumstances or under applicable federal, state or local laws.

Moosul Publishing, LLC
211 Miller Avenue
Mulvane, Kansas 67110
United States of America
(316) 214-8695
www.MoosulPublishing.com

Acknowledgements

There were a few years where I was convinced forms were a complete waste of time. Yet my instructors persisted and kept impressing upon me that being good at sparring just meant you were good at sparring. I had no idea what that meant.

Eventually I figured out what they were saying and must express my heartfelt gratitude to my instructors: **Bryan Robbins**, **Michael Proctor**, **Paul Hinkley**, and **Tony Tan Suan Hee**. Your generosity, your patience, and your training continues to guide my every step. What you told me about the importance of the traditional forms, the need to apply those forms, and the correct effort needed—many of the words in this book are straight from you.

Special acknowledgement to American Karate and Taekwondo Organization (AKATO) **Grandmaster Keith D. Yates**—the practitioner I aspire to be, and a leader I proudly follow.

I had intended to publish this book to commemorate AKATO's 40th anniversary in 2016, and to recognize the pivotal influence this organization has had in supporting me all these years, but the book took longer than expected to complete. I was lucky to have walked into an AKATO school while living in the Southwestern United States in the early 1990s. I could not have found a better martial arts family.

Sincere apologies to **Hanshi Tim White** for the grief I've given him as he's guided me into my senior ranks. His insistence that rank doesn't matter, is of course, correct. It doesn't.

And yet it does.

I am indebted to the inspiration provided by **Dr. Bruce D. Clayton**, **Kelly Worden**, **Dan Djurdjevic**, and my longtime friend **Stuart Anslow**. Their invaluable experience, body of work, and leadership has buoyed my motivation over many years.

My deepest appreciation to my crew—in no particular order—**Kelly Cox**, **Mark Lynn**, **Robert Woerner**, **Tony Tempesta**, **Forrest Littlejohn**, **Jon Alster**, **Will Senn**, **Joseph Battino**, **Meg Hinkley**, **Toby Threadgill**, **Dr. Tom Barry**, **Stephen Starnes**, **Erica Bollon**, **Dean Chapman**, **Gary Simpson**, **Peter Wong**, **Terence Bridgeman**, **Doug Spear**, **Peter James**, **Peter Zlatko Kitak**, **Nenad Djurdjevic**, **Debbie Clarke**, **Andrew Netes**, **Dragan Malesic**, **Vincent Cordeiro**, **Gawain Siu**, **Ørjan Nilsen**, **Samir Berardo**, **Eric San Jose**, **Patrick Saw**, **Ong Seow Hsiung**, **Hoo Kwok Chye** and **Will Just**—for the people you are, for your friendship, and for your unwavering support of my endeavors.

A special round of applause to:

Dr. Sanko Lewis @sooshimkwan for his tactical discussion on ITF Sine Wave. Soo Shim Kwan inspired content influences Application 3, "Changing Levels on the Opponent."

Nate Creevey @natecree for sharing content from the Russell Fallon Seminar at Blackwater Taekwon-Do Korean Australian Taekwon-Do Organisation (KATO). KATO inspired content can be seen in Application 5, "Springing the Trap."

Practical Method @practicalmethodaustralia for their online sharing. Master Chen Zhonghua's Practical Method (真不动) or "Matching Opponent with Rotation" inspired content influences Application 5, "Springing the Trap."

Johannes Regell youtube.com/@KissakiKaiSweden for sharing his Passai Boxing System content. Johannes Regell's content inspires Application 7, "Rising Fists Boxing System."

Mark Lynn @mark.lynn.3958 put so much work brainstorming the Figure 9 down block. This helped fine-tune content in Application 9, "Attack the Hip to Drop the Opponent."

WA Institute of Martial Arts as hosts of the Taira Bunkai Seminar 2018. Taira Masaji inspired content influences "Sweep the Leg (Then the Other Leg)."

Warmest thoughts to **Mireille Clark** for editing my first manuscript in 2005—that work was entirely premature but became a roadmap to the birth of "The JDK methodology." JDK, or Joong Do Kwan, is my school in Perth in Western Australia.

I must thank **Charlie Wildish** of **Bunkai Jutsu** for his article on Nov 3, 2017: "Interview with Colin Wee, 6th Dan TKD Master, Blogger, Youtuber and Soon to Be Author," available on his blog at BunkaiJutsu.com.

Acknowledgements to **Mike Swope** for his article "An Interview with Sabumnim Colin Wee," which appeared in *Totally Taekwondo*, Feb 2018, Issue 108; and also for his invitation to write a recommendation for Supreme Master Kim Bok-Man's photo history book, *Taekwon-Do: Origins of the Art: Bok Man Kim's Historical Photospective (1955-2015)*.

Acknowledgements once again to **Stuart Anslow** for his referencing *Fighting Heaven and Earth*, otherwise known as my premature manuscript, in *Ch'ang Hon Taekwon-do Hae Sul (Volume 1)*. Stuart is the editor of *Totally Tae Kwon Do* magazine in the UK (see TotallyTKD.com).

Much gratitude to artist and calligrapher **Chew Siew Kheng**, who created the beautiful Nam Seo Kwan scroll displayed herein, and to my friend **Pang Sze Yunn**, who organized its creation for me.

And lastly, a shout out to **Jeremy Lesniak** for the Nov 11, 2019 interview, "Episode 448 – Master Colin Wee," available on Whistlekick Martial Arts Radio (WhistleKickMartialArtsRadio.com).

Greetings to the friends who get what we do and enjoy the over-share in JDK Library on Facebook (facebook.com/groups/jdklibrary).

Joshua Lay and **Niaal Holder**—it's been my pleasure to be your instructor. More than that, you've helped me become the instructor I didn't know I could be. Thank you for sticking with it through times when even I didn't know what I was doing.

Editing and Layout	**Mike Swope**
Applications Photoshoot	**Lorna Baker**
	Oscar Barrett
	Joshua Lay
	Kaden Prowse
	Bethany Wee
Content Focus Group	**Joshua Lay**
	Roy Moore
Cover Artwork	**Nazar Horokhivskyi**

To my family—**Emmy**, **Wills**, and **MSB**. Where would I even be without your support and understanding? Emmy—I couldn't have done this without you.

Thank you to my **mum**, who has always read the manuscripts and praised them generously; I might still have to explain this all to you one day, mum.

And lastly, to the man who started me down the path of the warrior, my **dad**:

Bill Wee
Father of Archery in Singapore
1936 - 2015

Table of Contents

Foreword by Grandmaster Keith Yates 3

Part 1: Birth of the JDK Method

    Our Corner of the World............................... 5
    The Problem No One Talks About 7
    Learning in a Kata-Based Environment 15
    Breaking through to Training Secrets 21

Part 2: Applications

    Pattern Diagram for Bassai Dai 24-25

Application 1:
Spin the Opponent Off His Base 26
    General Application
    Alternate Applications:
        General Holding a Seal/Stamp
        Wrecking Ball
    Questions for Self-Study

Application 2:
Mid-Blocks Pattern Within a Pattern 34
    Part 1: Getting Past the Lead Guard
    Part 2: Blitz Attack
    Part 3: When Our Windshield Wiper Fails
    Part 4: Getting Past the Lead Guard Redux
    Additional Principles
    Questions for Self-Study

Application 3:
Changing Levels on the Opponent 46
    General Application
    Important Observations
    Questions for Self-Study

Application 4:
Knife Hand as Multi-Tool 52
    General Application
    A Note on Footwork
    Questions for Self-Study

Application 5:
Springing the Trap 58
    A Word About Traps
    General Application
    Questions for Self-Study

Application 6:
Destroy the Opponent's Base 64
    Turns & Takedowns in *Kata*
    Shuhari & Bassai Dai *Kata*
    General Application
    Explaining the Void
    Questions for Self-Study

Application 7:
Rising Fists Boxing System. 72
    Bassai's Chinese Influences
    General Application
    Alternate Application 1:
        Sink His Head into His Base
    Alternate Application 2:
        Extrapolation of the Spinning
        Dantian Throw
    Spinning *Dantian* Throw: The Oral
        Transmission of Body Mechanics
    Questions for Self-Study

Application 8:
Pushing & Pulling 82
    Aikido in the JDK
    General Application
    Aiki & Judo 101
    Questions for Self-Study

Application 9:
Attack the Hip to Drop the Opponent 88
    The Figure 9 Block – NOT an Arm Break
    General Application
    Inside the Opponent's Arms
    Outside the Opponent's Arms
    Questions for Self-Study

Application 10:
Mountain Strike Strips His Guard 94
    General Application
    Vertical + Horizontal Axes
    Questions for Self-Study

Application 11:
Big Scoop Limb Control 100
    General Application
    Inside the Arm
    Outside the Arm
    Regarding Knife Defense
    Questions for Self-Study

Application 12:
Sweep the Leg (Then the Other Leg) 108
    General Application
    Train for Failure
    The JDK If-Then-Else Protocol
    If Two Techniques Fail...
    If Our Third Technique Fails...
    If He Stutter-Steps Instead:
        Return of the Figure 9 Pile Driver
    Did We Mention Safety?
    Questions for Self-Study

Works Cited 120

An Interview with *Sabumnim* Colin Wee 122
    from *Totally Tae Kwon Do* Magazine

Foreword
by Grandmaster Keith Yates

Kata: Literally, "A shape that cuts into the earth," as in a "pattern" or "form."

My mother used to sew her own clothing. She would often go to the fabric store to buy not just bolts of cloth but also those really thin, paper patterns that she used to cut out shapes which she would then sew together to make a beautiful but still practical garment.

That, in essence, is the definition of a martial arts pattern, or *kata* in Japanese. An outline of various pieces that, when combined in the proper way, is not just a thing of physical beauty but also an efficient and practical series of self-defense movements and techniques. In fact, that's what the Japanese *kanji*, the Japanese character, actually indicates: a drawn-out pattern or "shape."

Colin Wee has delivered a masterful breakdown (*bunkai* in Japanese) of one of the most ubiquitous karate *kata* around. He has spent many hours dissecting individual sequences and showing their application in an in-close situation — what *kata* are actually designed for as opposed to sport-type sparring.

I have always been impressed with Colin's dedication to a deeper level of study and his refusal to just accept *kata* as merely a way to qualify for your next color belt. Indeed, this superficial mindset has often permeated the 21st century approach to karate, taekwondo, and even the Chinese arts.

We have to go back to the early 20th century to see what Gichin Funakoshi, one of the founders, said. "You may train for a long time, but if you merely move your hands and feet and jump up and down like a puppet, learning karate is not very different from learning a dance. You will never have reached the heart of the matter; you will have failed to grasp the quintessence of karate-do."

So here Colin presents the quintessence of Bassai *kata*. It is my hope that readers will spend time with the text and illustrations he presents to come to a greater understanding of the practical fundamentals and principles of not just this but all *kata*.

Funakoshi sensei would be pleased.

K. Yates

In Our Corner of the World

Grandmaster Keith D. Yates heads the American Karate and Tae Kwon Do Organization (AKATO). Under that umbrella, Mr. Yates' school, Nam Seo Kwan, carries a lineage exported out of Korea by Grandmaster Jhoon Rhee in 1956.

In writing a recommendation for *Taekwon-Do: Origins of the Art: Bok Man Kim's Historic Photospective (1955-2015)*, I describe this early era as "Taekwondo out to prove itself" with the most "audacious bare-knuckled, no holds barred practitioners" (Kim 255). In the

▲ Grandmaster Keith Yates formalized Nam Seo Kwan Tae Kwon Do in 1980.

When Grandmaster Rhee brought his martial art to the Southwestern United States in the 1950s, he would become the Father of American Tae Kwon Do. Only it wasn't yet Tae Kwon Do. It was *Tang Soo Do*, a Korean translation of the original meaning of Japanese *Karate*, literally "The Way of the China Hand." This history pre-dates the founding of both the International Taekwon-Do Federation (ITF) and the World Taekwondo Federation (WTF), and sets our lineage apart.

Tang Soo Do instructors taught Karate *kata*, i.e. Pyung Ahn 1–5, Tekki 1–3, Bassai and Jitte, and called what they did American Karate or Korean Karate. Grandmaster Rhee only started using the term Tae Kwon Do in 1962. Then in 1967 our practitioners adopted the ITF Ch'ang Hon *tuls*, or patterns, at the behest of General Choi Hong-Hi, the founder of Taekwon-Do.

Southwestern United States, this was taken to a whole new level, with "Texas Karate fighters considered to be the toughest 'Blood and Guts' fighters found anywhere in the U.S." (Worley).

The proximity of our lineage to Japanese and Okinawan arts persisted beyond the conversion to Korean forms. Grandmaster Yates' Nam Seo Kwan continued to practice the Chung Do Kwan forms, acquired elements of Japanese and Okinawan Karate, and incorporated aspects of Ju-Jutsu, a Japanese close-range combat art, and *Kobudo*, an Okinawan weapons-based system.

In 1996, Grandmaster Yates changed the name of his association to American Karate and Tae Kwon Do Organization for better representation of its base of multi-style practitioners. AKATO member schools "maintain a traditional but ecclectic approach to their martial practice" (Yates, "Brief History").

AKATO's traditional eclecticism works. While members respect one's lineage and system, they also express an openness seldom found elsewhere, teaching joint locks, throws and weapons alongside traditional Korean kicks (Yates, "Brief History").

This eclecticism was alive and well when I walked into an AKATO member club in the early 1990s. Its openness was clearly evident. Black belts from multiple styles participated in our training sessions. They were well-adjusted and friendly, all happy to be guided by my instructor. Such is not common in the martial arts world. Styles, even schools, typically kept to themselves and rarely interacted, except perhaps when competing at a tournament.

On Saturday mornings in our corner of the world, a dozen or so black belts would line-up at the head of the room. A handful studied Grandmaster Yates' Tae Kwon Do, others might practice Wado Ryu or Kempo Karate, and my other instructor would occasionally visit and represent Shotokan.

We couldn't help but engage in conversations and discussions in our training mosh pit. While we dissected techniques and varied our tactics, we were also interested in each black belt and what they brought from their base style, which of them were learning other systems, and who planned to attend my teacher's Aikido session later that morning or the Kobudo program held each month.

I benefited hugely from this eclectic approach, and the happiness and contentment I felt fueled my practice for many years after I left the U.S. Even the naming of my school acknowledges the philosophy of AKATO: *Joong Do Kwan* translates to "School of the Middle Way." It is the mid-point between the rich heritage linking us to Japan, Okinawa, and China, and the equally important modern advances that improve our practice and our well-being.

AKATO instructors set me on this path, a trajectory I've tried to take to the nth level. I've not always known what it is that I have sought. But I've done my best to remain true of heart and pure of purpose. ■

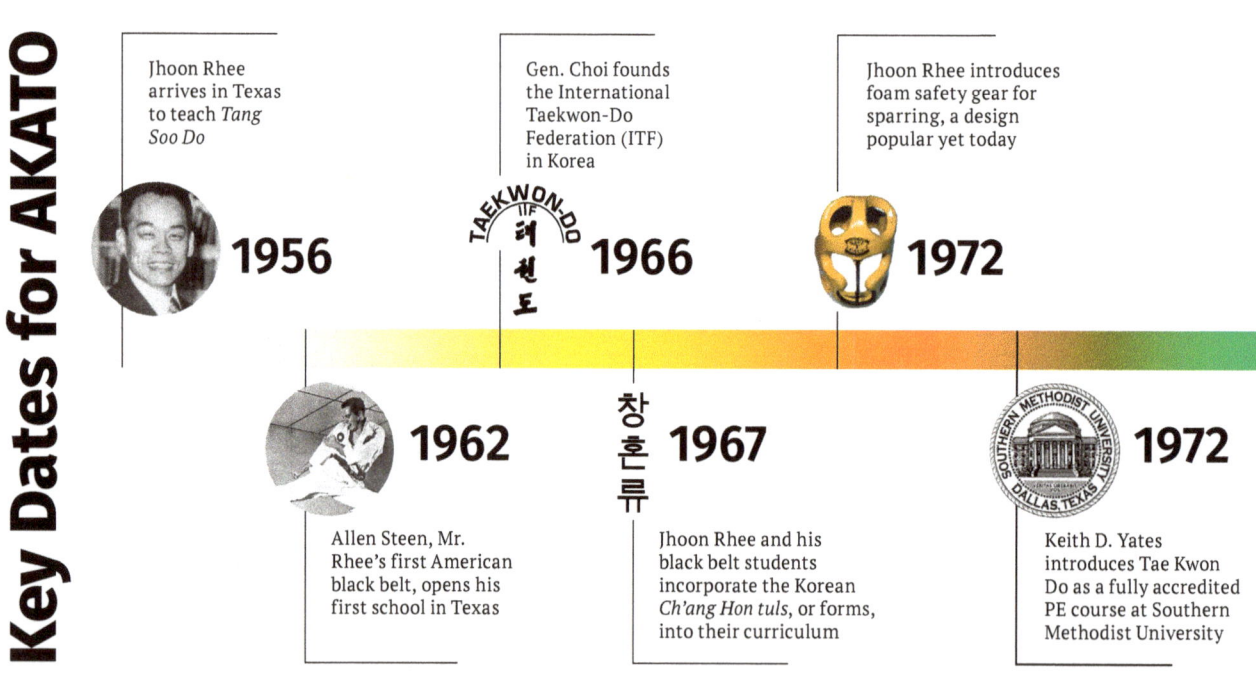

Key Dates for AKATO

- **1956** — Jhoon Rhee arrives in Texas to teach *Tang Soo Do*
- **1962** — Allen Steen, Mr. Rhee's first American black belt, opens his first school in Texas
- **1966** — Gen. Choi founds the International Taekwon-Do Federation (ITF) in Korea
- **1967** — Jhoon Rhee and his black belt students incorporate the Korean *Ch'ang Hon tuls*, or forms, into their curriculum
- **1972** — Jhoon Rhee introduces foam safety gear for sparring, a design popular yet today
- **1972** — Keith D. Yates introduces Tae Kwon Do as a fully accredited PE course at Southern Methodist University

The Problem No One Talks About
Birth of the JDK Method

I had an online conversation—circa 2011—with a young black belt *karateka*.

He was respectful and interested and shared video of himself in a sparring competition. He was taller than his opponent, with solid sparring experience, reflexes, and a longer reach. He was clearly the more talented of the two fighters, and dominated the exchange. His opponent had lackluster strategy and poor conditioning, and was getting demolished.

While I enjoyed his video, I was curious about his fight plan. I asked what he would have done differently if he had fought a more worthy opponent. An opponent who was not disadvantaged by height, reach or skill. What would he do if he had faced an opponent of the caliber of Mike Tyson? His answers gave me insight into his training.

He first said he would try harder. Then he said he would endure through the counter attack. Finally, he said he'd have to rely on divine intervention!

The young black belt's answer was not wrong—he's entitled to his approach.

I could not help but contrast his answer to the time when I was a young black belt. I kept notes on every sparring session I had. Through the week following, I'd explore combinations in my mind.

I was desperate to level up against those opponents when I was next paired with them. My young black belt way of thinking told me I needed a store of combinations tailored to my opponents. I wanted to know which combos worked well, which of them needed to be fine-tuned or binned, and how to better play off my various striking skills with those combos to make them more effective.

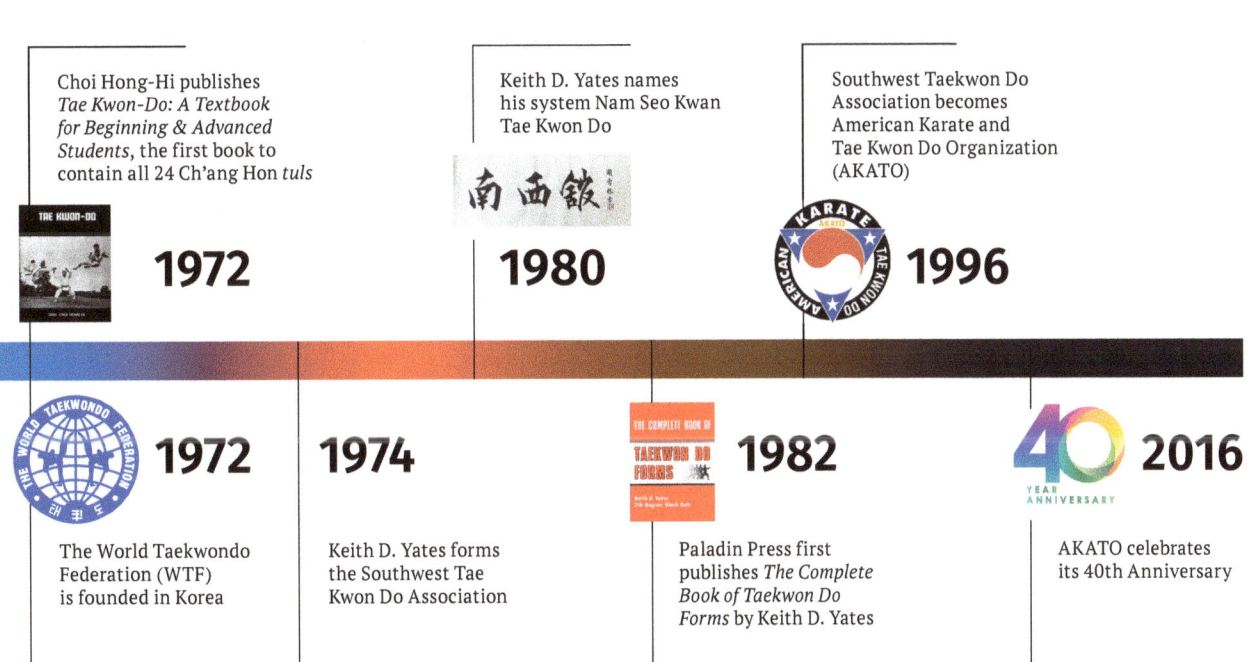

If I was growing up in the 21st Century with access to YouTube, I would have expanded my research to explore boxing greats and breakdowns of their fights. I would consume any media from any combat sport tradition. And I would be seeking mentors who could provide the insight that I sought. Insight that would answer the questions that modern students need to ask of their traditional lineage and training methodology:

- How do you progress as a martial artist if you solely train like a beginner and think fitness will win the day?
- How do you adapt to challenges if you only train using repetition of fixed set patterns?
- How do you acquire fight IQ without the spirit of collaboration?

* * *

I trained in Texas with AKATO until I graduated in 1995 and returned to Singapore. In 2000, I moved with my wife, Emmeline, to Perth, Australia, and worked as Chief Information Officer for an online insurance broker. I started my small training group, instigated by colleagues in my department.

By 2002, after 19 years of training, and not long after establishing that little training group, I felt lost.

I taught what I knew worked and had fun establishing a group of students, but I was 10,000 miles from the mother ship. I didn't have my crew dissecting tactics, discussing variations, or looking out for me. I felt inadequate. And I was on the verge of throwing in the towel.

Up to that point I was a decent martial artist. In my youth, I had started in an eclectic Chinese system, received my black belt at the end of high school, was drafted, and when my service to my country was over, left to attend college in the Southwestern United States. In college, it was my luck to step into an AKATO school situated on campus.

There I started training American Karate and Aikido. The learning curve was steep. The training I had when I was younger was appropriate for a junior black belt, but training in the U.S. made me feel like I was being schooled time-and-time-again.

I loved it. Each week I had the luxury to attend three or four official classes, two sparring sessions, and go to the gym about four to five times a week.

The training was distinctly different from my first black belt. In American Karate, we would mostly follow a Three-K (aka 3K) approach to training. This is similar to most other modern hard style training sessions. The 3K approach originated from Japanese Karate training methodology: *kihon* (基本), or basic techniques; *kata* (型), prearranged sequences of techniques; and *kumite* (組手), sparring.

Aikido, on the other hand, was so different that I struggled with regular classes until I had the opportunity to join the Aikido PE program offered through my university, where I was happy to run through the official beginner 9th *kyu* program.

As one might guess, training in martial arts was a major part of my college experience, and leaving the Southwestern United States left a huge hole in the center my being. Of course, when it eventually came time to start my own group, I wanted to ensure my students had the same experience I received in the U.S. I wanted to do right by them, keep the legitimacy of our lineage, and feel assured they could hold their own in the ring. We chose to call our group the Joong Do Kwan (JDK).

I began to pull a syllabus together for my students – and all my doubts of which I had been blissfully unaware rose immediately to the surface. I discovered that the

Internet is a deep and dark place, full of misgivings about hard style martial arts and keyboard warriors painfully lambasting the deficiencies of black belts.

Instead of being confident in my own skills, I became filled with self-doubt. Certainly, not everything I had trained and built was useless. But on the other hand, I had a growing dread for everything that I couldn't do, and for having none of the answers or solutions for my hard style '"sins" for which those keyboard warriors were castigating me.

I was at the precipice of giving up but felt compelled through sheer stubbornness alone to try and take a mature view of the work I had completed and the work I yet needed to complete. I needed to identify my system's strengths and weaknesses; to reconcile the damning deficiencies; and do it all without betraying my lineage and myself. Fortunately, Perseverance is one of the Five Tenets of Taekwondo, and its corollary is stubbornness, of which I have an abundance.

To my ironic delight, the source of my emotional pain—the Internet—was also the tool for me to begin to find solutions and answers. I was able to reach out to like-minded practitioners and touch base with those who were also seeking their own truths. I connected with some very clever martial artists, all of whom I have named in the acknowledgments. In two decades, neither my gratitude for their help nor our friendships have diminished.

3K Training: *Kihon, Kata* & *Kumite*

The meandering path I took searching for answers brought me back time and again to the hard style training approach of modern Karate, an approach which was introduced and institutionalized in the early 20th century when combative systems from Okinawa were brought over to the Japanese mainland. Japanese *karateka* formalized these fighting systems and created a fitness and training program used initially for students studying at Japanese universities. These pioneering efforts were then later supported by Japan's burgeoning war machine as a way to strengthen and prepare young men for military service.

Everyone likes a bit of structure. In 1.5 to 2 hours, instructors can run through a warmup (20 min); fundamental drills (30 min); practice patterns or learn

▲ The traditional 3K approach to hard-style training is easy to understand and formulaic, and can literally be transported to any location without mental gymnastics. It works well for training large classes of beginners, as originally used in the Japanese military; choreographing demos; and promoting safe competition. It can be overused, however, when instructors rely on it exclusively for senior students and black belts.

new ones (30 min); and then engage in free, stylized or one step *kumite* (30 min).

This new approach was easy to understand, formulaic, and transportable. Such an approach meant aspiring instructors who wanted to set up their own martial arts school could do so without the prerequisite of creative thinking or mental gymnastics. They simply taught what they had learned the way they had learned it. 3K training became wildly popular and was soon exported to countries such as Korea prior to World War II. American soldiers stationed in Japan and Okinawa after the War also took Karate and the 3K method home with them. Karate took root in like manner in other countries around the world.

The complaint of long-time martial artists is that 3K training is too rigid and its prescriptive approach too contrived for the real world. We agree that 3K is a really solid approach for beginners and intermediates. But its advantages end there.

Seasoned martial artists know that 3K works well for training large classes of beginners, choreographing demos, and promoting safe competition, but they also know that the training is duplicitous. While students believe they are training in a traditional or complete martial system, in reality they are immersed only in the staged, choreographed movements of 3K training. As these students become instructors, they continue to teach using the traditional 3K method. *Ad infinitum*. Perhaps for convenience. Perhaps because it is easy. Perhaps due to indoctrination. Perhaps for sentimentality.

Like millions of other *karateka*, I was trained in the traditional prescribed manner by some very good martial artists and fight instructors, and I was an aspiring instructor who taught the 3K program, trying to protect the legitimacy of my system and lineage. I was desperate for my students to become as skilled and proficient as I believed I had become. So I kept things the same to be respectful to my seniors, as do thousands of instructors worldwide. That method, after all, had propelled me this far.

Yet by 2002 I had a sense of growing disenchantment. I began to recognize that we were not testing new skills, not developing an intellectual curiosity which occurs as people cross train, and ignoring the idea that students can actually become better than their teacher.

I admit that when I started, I was complicit in formalizing a traditional 3K practice. I had left the womb of AKATO's mothership, was taking my first steps as an instructor alone, and was adamant to hold on to the system which I had been gifted. The 3K approach to training was what I had been brought up on, and its ease of use felt like divine providence. I knew I could do this without thinking! But I know now, without all those black belts trying to make sense of what we were practicing, I was simply transmitting fixed set patterns. And probably not doing a great job at that.

I also admit that I still depend on the 3K structure. As a training approach, especially for beginning and intermediate students, the *kihon/kata/kumite* study is perfect to lay foundational skills. I am convinced, however, that it can be and is often overused. How do instructors justify its use exclusively for senior students? I believe goal-oriented instructors will eventually recognize that a loosening of that rigid structure is needed at some point for a student's continued growth and development.

Finding Our Way

Of course, when I began the search to remedy my growing sense of disenchantment, I hadn't yet developed this larger perspective. I only saw things from the inside, from a single perspective. My new-found friends, and our discussions and efforts at research, would eventually squash my overwhelming doubt. A team effort, as they say, was needed, and little did I realize this game would require extra innings.

The disconnected voices on the Internet and my own inexperience meant a lot of our early work kept our wheels spinning but often led us to dead ends. For instance, I spent almost two years trying to spreadsheet all relevant knowledge, then pairing that knowledge with techniques found in our patterns. Some of this work has persisted, so these efforts weren't all in vain.

I realized eventually that I couldn't easily adapt the skills I had or conjure up skills I didn't have. I also noticed that many of the techniques and/or sequences in the patterns were simply orphaned, unpaired within my spreadsheet. I came to understand that appending more words to techniques wasn't going to create additional value.

As we continued to trawl the Internet, we noticed there was an ever-increasing focus on application training, and more and more application videos began to pop up on the sites we regularly researched. Were these videos intended to circumvent the limitations of 3K training? Or were these application videos a circular justification for *kata*-based training?

As with all things, the quality of YouTube martial arts applications varied wildly, from stilted performances to rare gems. They often promised more, but many were no more than examples of the evergreen one-step sparring techniques we had always taught colored belts. Overall, they were generally disappointing.

So the dread of not knowing what I felt I should know persisted, my thoughts now compounded by an anxiety of realizing I must do something to change the way I trained my students. I needed to evolve the 3K methodology to ensure my students' continuing growth, but I had no clear roadmap of how to do that.

The only lifeline came from my background as a coach and competitor in archery.

In a sporting environment, a coach can increase the intensity or difficulty of competition to stress test experienced athletes by swapping opponents with greater or lesser skill, increasing or decreasing team members as appropriate (if it is a team sport), and by reducing the capacity of an opponent or opponents to act with specific limitations, such as the clichéd arm tied behind one's back. As a training exercise, coaches simply change the training environment in some manner to make it more difficult for athletes. Or to just see how a particular training scenario might work. All to improve the performance of athletes.

With that logic, I started modifying the parameters of almost all 3K exercises used in my classes. This was a way to explore what might work better for training and to force everyone to adapt to whatever changes were presented. Honestly, though, I had no clue how things would pan out, whether any of the things we tried would make my students better, or whether my students would all simply quit and leave me the laughing stock of the martial arts world.

To my surprise, most of my students in those early years kept coming back to class, session after session, possibly drawn by the demanding physical skills, or our discussions about what it was that we were doing and how best to go about doing it.

To use correct Japanese vernacular, we were trying to gain clarity of the *bunkai* within our patterns by deconstructing them. At the same time, our attempts to inject tactical skills from our contact sparring back into the patterns germinated into the study of *oyo,* of application, within them.

Bunkai (分解): A Japanese term which refers to the "deconstruction of a form." It is a supplemental teaching aid, a literal translation of the form which supports learning the movements within the pattern by showing how a technique finds its level or mark and how the body is structured during the movements. Instructors rely on *bunkai* when emphasizing the sequence of techniques since *bunkai* is merely their representation, or interpretation, of a sequence within *kata*. *Bunkai* explains and reinforces the *kata*, and some *bunkai* may be worthwhile tactically, but it need not be so. It can simply be a legacy leftover from the 3K approach to training. As such, it is performed by rote. *Bunkai*, however, might still be useful in certain training exercises. The Korean equivalent is *bunhae* (분해).

Oyo (応用): A Japanese term which means "application." Often used synonymously with *bunkai*, and as such pertains to pragmatic skills that must be applied from the *kata*. Applications are often considered a "step up" from *bunkai* because they are techniques applied by concept and/or tactic and not necessarily by mechanical rote, or because the instructor has said so (though that is how *bunkai* becomes *oyo*). It's not necessary for an *oyo* to be more sophisticated than *bunkai*. *Oyo* may be irrespective of sequence or timing or level. The concept could be related to the associated *bunkai* in any given circumstance. Or it could be taken from another *bunkai*. The best applications are tactically useful to the practitioner and always consider the resistance of a non-compliant opponent in a dynamic situation. The Korean equivalent is *eungyong* (응용).

Breaking Through: The JDK Method

It has been some time since I was that young black belt. In the intervening years, the question for me has changed from "What combos do I need to beat the opponent?" to "What skills did the architects of our system have? And what did they want us to understand when they designed these *kata*?"

As we searched to relieve our discontent, we found ourselves returning to our lineage, wondering about the *karateka* behind the *kata*, and what training was like before the *kata*. This wasn't some wishful thinking on our part to discover fantastical or superhuman abilities lost in the mists of time. The more we deconstructed the *kata* and understood its role in our training environment, the more we felt connected to the human condition that underpins every *kata*.

The JDK Method ➤

The JDK Method encourages practitioners to explore movements and techniques found within their patterns to discover the conditions under which they can be successfully used to defend themselves and the conditions under which they fail. In the JDK Method, students train as both attacker and defender to understand how an attacker is affected by the defender's response and ways in which he may press the attack. In this way, students learn to impede, restrict or otherwise lead an aggressor towards predictable attacks. Any attack may have multiple useful responses, as shown here.

Starting Position | Application A | Application B | Application C

I knew it was important for the *kata* or the pattern set to be our syllabus. The syllabus frames the training that students need. It becomes a framework from which you hang your skills, structure your understanding, and extrapolate from limited knowledge.

The *kata* is here as part of our legacy. We've learned it. And as we keep asking questions of it, sometimes the answers appear, albeit slowly. The biggest breakthrough after our spreadsheeting extravaganza occurred with Tekki Shodan some time before 2010. Tekki has the simplest *embusen*, a Japanese term which describes a *kata*'s starting point and lines of movement across the ground or floor. Tekki's fairly simple movements are mirrored on both sides. It is not a difficult *kata*, yet it is one of the more fundamental patterns from Okinawa.

Our breakthrough with Tekki was that the same techniques in the pattern could be applied to a strike coming from the opponent's lead hand or the opponent's secondary tool. And, fundamental to Joong Do Kwan's mode of thinking, they could still be applied if we anticipated the "wrong" hand.

Most other *kata* from our lineage have about 40 or so techniques sequenced together. Often, when Joong Do Kwan (JDK) workshops a singular technique or series from a pattern, we might go through a dozen variations or more when anticipating the opponent's counters. As we put a *kata* through its paces, we might look at over 400 combinations of techniques! We video some of our work and share it. But that is not definitive. The way we approach training requires us to continually read and assess what the opponent is going to do so that we may respond appropriately.

The tactics that stick, the tactics that we return to, are those that make sense for our crew. That is, the training methodology needs to consider the practitioner's range of skills, what the practitioner prefers to use, and how easy it is for the practitioner to make any given tactic work. This is what JDK does really well – we receive immediate feedback from the student in our environment and tune our system based off our collective abilities.

We eventually named our unique approach to training. We call it the JDK Method.

It is not a syllabus in the traditional sense. Sometimes we just bypass 3K. We might go for months without sparring. Or months doing no patterns. And we sometimes only incorporate minimal fundamentals in warmups. We could run basically the same technique sequence for weeks on end in a two-man drill. For instance, the double block sequence from Bassai – see Application #2 – stuck with us for 6-9 months of the year. So we came to class and kept drilling variations upon variations upon variations, inspired by literally two blocks.

Drilling down into the application helps us work the skills which are undeveloped by 3K: distancing, timing, angles, anticipation of the opponent's initiative, receiving and interpreting kinesthetic feedback, and close quarter exchanges. Increasing non-compliance in a collaborative environment means we are able to workshop a wide range of tactics. These may include some soft-style skills or techniques that are unrelated to the original *bunkai*. Without ego, we assess the situations as they unfold and apply our growing understanding to meet them. If an application doesn't work, it gets parked – sometimes for a long time. As we gain insight from what works for us, we may eventually pull it back into our training. If we do, we mention it as we practice. We visualise. We practice it with other *bunkai*. We assimilate it. We learn to use it.

The Lessons Herein

Kata for us is a gift of something special. Each *kata* is its own fighting system. The architects weren't simply handing over a sequence of 40 or so beginner or standalone techniques – this is a very narrow view of *kata*. The pioneers of *kata* wanted to tell us something. And we've been trying to find out what exactly that is by studying their worldview, using *kata* as a lens.

The applications inspired by Bassai Dai and presented in this book hint at influences from Okinawan Karate, Japanese systems, Korean arts, and Chinese martial arts. We don't claim mastery over these systems – but many good systems and teachers will share similar skills which can be distilled from patterns taught and practiced in other systems.

The lessons in this book are not limited by labels, styles or the techniques themselves. On my Instagram profile, I say I'm less about "style" and more about "class." While tongue-in-cheek, this means that good, solid concepts can be found seeded throughout all good schools. The JDK Method, while it works for us, is not the one, true way. Other systems also feature pragmatic and "real" training. We have no doubt that, with an open mind and open heart, students will be able to find such jewels within any system they study.

There is nothing wrong with preserving lineage and taking pride in the traditions within one's chosen art. And, finally, there is nothing wrong with family-friendly sport-focused competition. Each has its place.

To catch a glimpse into the worldview of those early martial art pioneers, we need to have clarity about what we are trying to accomplish. We need to 'empty' our cup. But we don't empty it of our existing skills. We empty ourselves of our preconceptions, our bias, and incomplete assumptions. With new insight, we add to our base and build our foundation. Then perhaps we will also see that everything those martial pioneers wished to teach only began with *kata*. It does not end with *kata*.

This thinking leads to correct *doryoku* (努力), or effort. It is not limited to physical hardship or simple mimicry as the be-all and end-all of training. A person's "style" is not a demo or a cosmetic feature. Rather, style is a training methodology which develops a particular set of skills. The fixation on basics, without seeking tactical skill, is misspent *doryoku*. This is often seen in practitioners who have not yet taken a deep dive into their system.

If you, as a practitioner, suspect there is more that can be done with *kata*—if you want to avoid pie-in-the-sky *bunkai*, to ask and answer questions that will improve your combative skill, to build a game plan which does not rely on divine inspiration or providence, and to deeply explore tactical ideas – *Breaking Through* is the resource for you.

This book contains concepts to inspire you beyond your first black belt and questions to enrich your own path of self-discovery. *Breaking Through* is a celebration of traditional training.

I invite you to ask those questions that are important to you. And your lineage. ■

Learning in a Kata-Based Environment

When I was a young black belt, I was hugely interested in developing my sparring skills. I was obsessed with the semi-contact exchange, the thrill of mixing it up with a live opponent, the immediacy of the encounter, getting into a flow state, and I loved seeing my skills grow. I would not have admitted it then, but I was hooked on the adrenaline rush.

Kata, in contrast, lacked that appeal. When it came time to practice my patterns, I had to don a poker face, compose myself, and attempt to learn something I found hard to invest myself in emotionally.

If only someone had explained to me back then that persisting with *kata* and traditional techniques was the way to develop real skill in the martial arts. In my teachers' defense, they did keep pushing me to learn the forms, to depend on them when I was preparing to leave the mothership, and they did say "being good at sparring only means you are good at sparring." Is that enough, however, to convince a young black belt that the skills he prizes in his youth will not lead him to break through? That what seemed the less exciting area of martial study is how continued growth happens?

But *kata* as a structure for knowledge is not an effective sales pitch to a young black belt.

Kata, as noted earlier, refers to a predetermined sequence of movements and techniques brought together in a form or pattern to teach useful skills. The *kanji* for *kata* (型) represents an opening in the ground. *Kata* is a mold or model that can shape your growth. As Grandmaster Yates says, it's an outline. An outline that doesn't limit but helps structure one's growing knowledge base. Ideally, all *kata* by definition features training that develops some skillset of value to students.

Unfortunately, there are organizations which advertise that they don't practice *kata* or feel it is important in their training environment. Yet they still practice *kata*. Irrespective of how anti-*kata* a group might be, these very same organizations at some point will include predetermined sequences of techniques or drills in their training. These drills are *kata*. And like all *kata*, these drills develop skills important to their students.

As a traditional instructor, I might seem flippant regarding the fidelity of a *kata*'s *bunkai* and *oyo*. That I may seem more likely to choose my own flip-book-ending for the applications I teach. Nothing can be farther from the truth. The pattern set is a cornerstone of our practice, created by a skilled architect who desired to share his knowledge with others through *kata*.

Kata, unfortunately, is a naturally limited medium which transmits physical movements only. The student, to transcend the granularity of technique, must therefore interpret the language of *kata* to learn its lessons. In other words, *kata* instructs by and through the insights which the student draws, or infers, from their practice.

In summary, at JDK we understand that *kata* practice is more than a stringing together of basic techniques, that one can get immediate tactical value from practicing and studying *kata*, and that continued training in *kata* or any deconstructed sub-parts is one method by which one acquires pragmatic combative skill. *Kata* practice for the sake of stringing together basic techniques offers little value to a student's martial education.

Shuhari

No discussion of *kata* would be complete without the Japanese concept of *Shuhari* (守破離). *Shuhari* are "the stages of learning to mastery" in a *kata*-based learning environment ("Shuhari"):

1. *Shu* extols students to follow the form;
2. *Ha* to vary the form;
3. *Ri* to leave the form to find its true lessons.

Following the form isn't about mindlessly performing techniques in sequence. *Shu* prompts the student to understand the conditions and situations in which the form works.

I have taught women's self-defense for many years. I tell the participants that they will leave class, go home, and immediately want to try the techniques out on a male friend, brother, or partner. That person, however, is not the best opponent for several reasons. He expects some form of painful technique, he doesn't want to get hurt, and he's looking for what has been learned so that he may negate or counter it. I emphasize to the self-defense participants that they need to recreate the exact same conditions used in class for their new skills to work. They simply do not have enough combative or self-defense experience otherwise.

This is the underlying basis of *shu*. It's challenging to understand how techniques work because students don't yet have the requisite exposure to combative exchanges.

To gain knowledge to better follow the form, students should seek information from a variety of sources, such as books, YouTube, and senior students. How do people successfully bring parts of the form into their practice? What kind of assumptions do they make? Do they freestyle it in *kumite*?

When students truly "follow the form," it centers them and improves their ability to react most effectively under duress.

When a student varies the form, i.e. *ha*, it isn't about varying the technique for the sake of having a hundred different ways of performing the same thing. It is about varying the technique based on the opponent. How fast is gap closing going to happen? What's the angle of entry of the attack? Will the strike be launched from the left, right or front? What's the setup?

When the student varies the form, the focus is on the reading and countering of a dynamic non-compliant opponent, who is bent on besting every initiative. A student may try harder with a single technique, and the student may seek divine intervention, but neither measure is likely to succeed if the technique simply doesn't work for the circumstance because they don't have the experience to read an opponent's initiative.

Students don't learn how to read an opponent by performing *kata* solo at home. Students need to work against live opponents and accumulate kinesthetic understanding. Students gain this physical feedback through one-step sparring, self-defense scenario training, and even by holding the power shield for opponents. Students kinetically feel how an opponent reacts to their techniques, observe how opponents move, and learn as their experience grows.

When a student varies the form, they acquire sensitivity to better read an opponent.

Lastly, leaving the form to find its true lessons, i.e. *ri*, is not about abandoning the *kata*. I know some modern combatives or reality-based practitioners who espouse pressure testing and scenario training over *kata* training. They "go hard or go home." Don't get me wrong. I admire many aspects of their training philosophy. However, I have observed that students in those systems often struggle to reach the ability of their teachers. They acquire good skills quickly but experience a ceiling to their growth equally quickly. Unfortunately, most trainees would find it hard to break through and get past this stagnation. Quality can't be pressure tested into the learning curve!

Compare this to expert level traditionalists who have trained in the "old ways." They're not out to prove themselves, not trying to get to the finish line first. Yet they have phenomenal control of three-dimensional space, of the parameters of movement, and of the void on the ground that the opponent will soon fill.

These are masters who have acquired such effectiveness it's hard to identify the techniques they have used. They flow because they no longer see the form as a technical repository. To them *kata* is the start of how to understand the world they inhabit. They use it to understand strategy and tactics. They see its structure and flow in and out of its limits. And they would be bewildered at the thought that modern *karateka* would only use the form as a tool to grade up and nothing more.

Let me speak directly for a moment.

As you become adept and gain insight, you may start to realize that your simple *kata* can be used to address weaknesses in pedagogy, to view flow in three-dimensional space, or to get a rarefied view of your combative system.

This doesn't mean you have transcended or escaped it as a mnemonic device. It doesn't mean that the *kata* has become irrelevant. It doesn't mean you are better than the *kata*. it just means you have recognized the *kata* as a launchpad and are now gaining a perspective that was not available to you before.

"Leaving the form to find its true lessons" is simply an acknowledgment that the *kata* is more than the sum of its parts.

The learning journey as described by *shuhari* is a cycle. You may follow the form, vary the form, and return to following the form. Or you may follow, vary, leave the form, and return to follow the form once you acquire additional insight. You may dwell on certain areas more than others. And your progress may not be as steady as it was when you were a practitioner fresh-on-the-path.

You won't gain knowledge all at once, or at the same rate. You might have to dwell on some areas longer than others. You might discover you aren't so good at this at all and depend on more experienced practitioners to share their insights. It should be clear, however, that an inquisitive attitude and an open mind is vital to succeed in a *kata*-based training environment. When there is no freedom to "play," *kata* becomes useless as a receptacle of knowledge.

Translating *Kata* to Application Training

Shuhari might help when sifting through the detritus found on YouTube. Does the bunkai complement a *kata*-based training environment? Does it help one acquire a better understanding of the conditions and situations in which the *kata* works? Does it help to improve the assessment of the opponent? Or is it just a standalone addition?

So important is such deliberation that the founder of Shotokan Karate, Gichin Funakoshi, exhorted all practitioners to "be constantly mindful, diligent, and resourceful, in your pursuit of the Way." He penned that as his ultimate tenet in *Shotokan Nijū Kun* (松濤館二十訓), or "Shotokan's Twenty Instructions," ("Nijū kun").

When I first began to embrace *shuhari* and use it to address our practice at Joong Do Kwan, I assessed everything I had learned and everything I thought I knew of the martial arts. I didn't reject my past simply

▲ *Kata* today is typically a solo enterprise. But it should not always be so. Students need to practice the movements of *kata* so they become fluent with the techniques. That is true. But this is only the first step to master any *kata*. According to the concept of *shuhari*, there are three stages to mastering a form: *shu*, *ha* and *ri*. Unfortunately, in most modern schools, students rarely progress beyond "following the form."

out of spite or the belief that the training was inferior. To embrace *shuhari*, I had to understand what it was that we actually practiced.

I turned my training group into an ongoing experiment. We assessed and innovated every training drill, every exercise, every lesson. In those early days, I had no idea how things would turn out. Some things stuck. Things that didn't were parked. In truth, we spun our wheels on many things, and there were long stretches of time where we weren't going anywhere very fast. More than once I thought I would lose credibility along with all my students. Why would they stick around if I couldn't verbalize exactly what we were looking for?

Our breakthrough didn't come all at once. It happened after we stopped trying to desperately interpret every phenomenon within the pattern. Like many others on YouTube, we started out with a huge obligation to append something to each technique in our *kata*. Why are they strung out in this particular sequence? What do they accomplish? Was the preceding technique a key to its interpretation? What happens after that sequence? Was there a turn somewhere? Was it done slowly and deliberately? We looked for any clue that would help us interpret every little thing in the *kata*. In itself, that wasn't such a bad way to spend time.

We started making inroads when we stopped being so micro, so technique-focused, and started addressing the needs of the student. Yes, we made some progress when we looked for applications from the technique sequences themselves, but our breakthrough really started happening when the focus became the student, the person who might need the *kata*'s help to survive an attack, rather than the techniques. He or she would be under duress, facing an impending threat, so we began to focus on the *kata*'s fighting concepts.

It was at this point we felt the architect of the *kata* begin to speak directly to us.

The technician has an opponent, He needs to guess what the opponent is going to do, but he is human, and can make mistakes. While the ability to preempt and foretell can be trained, his read of the situation is not guaranteed, so how well he performs or recovers depends on his training.

The instructor's applications and drills need to help the student guess what is coming. If the student's guess is incorrect, the application needs to adapt to the variation in the attack. And if the student's adaptation likewise hits resistance, or "a dead end," the student needs a Plan B, a counter for the counter.

Eventually, a good instructor will realize that every application and every technique will encounter opposition at every step and that training must be prepared to deal with an opponent who actively opposes every initiative. We always need a Plan B.

Copying Iain Abernathy's cool takedown, or anyone else's technique or combo, does not qualify as applications training. In our training environment, we always assume a stalemate, or an active opposition, and provide workarounds. It is a continuous cycle.

As we focused on our students' needs, our applications training experienced a paradigm shift. The student-centric approach encouraged—insisted—that we take content as needed from any of our patterns. Our *kata*-based training environment was never about limiting ourselves to any single *kata*. When we workshopped skills, we would draw from our entire repertoire of Chinese, Okinawan, Japanese and Korean patterns with impunity. We would vary the attack. Introduce other counters. Return back to the *kata*. And workshop our lesson to the nth degree.

Ultimately, when we talk about a "complete lesson" in JDK, it is inspired by a sequence in one *kata*. The packaged lesson is created from multiple perspectives, anticipating what the opponent might do, studying the techniques our students prefer, and preparing ourselves to read the next inevitable opposing initiative in the attack. This is all credited back to the original sequence which inspired the lesson, the impetus for all our work.

How Many Variations Is Too Many?

The student as the center of focus means we're not pushing an agenda to justify the use of *kata*. We want *kata* to work for our students, not the other way around. Because we didn't institutionalize any single way of doing things, we soon noticed that certain follow up techniques were used more frequently than others and realized that students favored certain combos to improve efficiency.

Why were some techniques used more frequently than others?

Because that's the purpose of practice. As we practice, our brain translates physical movement into memory. This translation, in the beginning, requires conscious effort, but as we repeat movements, the brain reinforces the memory each time until it becomes automatic, entirely bypassing conscious thought. This phenomenon significantly improves performance as the brain simultaneously processes information and moves the body.

We dubbed these favored fundamental skills the "JDK Library." Using them naturally frees up mental space so the technician can better read the opponent and gauge the situation. These are far from the handful of combos I used as a young black belt all those years ago. For one, the JDK Library is about what works as we bait the opponent to fight our fight. And second, we test multiple lines of tactics to find the best plug and play solutions.

Sometimes when we demonstrate applications to other groups the things we show may seem overwhelming or spectacular. That's because to share skills trained in an if-then-else style takes practitioners way beyond a literal demonstration of movements in *kata*. The technique sequence in *kata* could be the inspiration to train a certain *something*; after that, that *something* is taken to the end of its knowledge cycle, worked to the nth degree. That is how we understand Funakoshi's 13th precept, *tekki ni yotte tenka seyo* (敵に因って轉化せよ), prompting *karateka* to "make adjustments according to the opponent" ("Nijū kun").

As we work *kata* like this, every application need not be different. The JDK Library isn't a list of thousands upon thousands of techniques. No human practitioner—from any time period—can learn or be expected to train like this.

We want to reuse knowledge as much as possible. Anyone who's spent time with our practice will see sequences of applications used again and again. We "plug and play" them as needed. This is not lazy training; it is intelligent training.

Kata training for us became live training. It was no longer a repetitive choreographed routine of lifeless techniques. We always knew *kata* complemented the traditional oral transmission of knowledge. However, only when we started to use *kata* in the manner described here did it become the powerful mnemonic device it was engineered to be.

The more we communed with *kata*, the more we identified with the *kata*'s architects and their human condition. Across time and space, they began to speak to us, inviting us to contribute our own voice and apply the framework they left for us. ∎

◀ Joong Do Kwan was invited in 2014 to share portions of their syllabus with Taekwondo Kidokwan Perth, an ITF school whose training style differed from the burgeoning JDK Method. JDK covered applications from Chulgi/Tekki, disruption of center of gravity, simple takedowns, defenses against kicks, distancing, elbow strike flow drills, and sparring methods. JDK is honored to have been asked back to Kidokwan many times since. The insight acquired through the JDK Method does not ask practitioners to reject their identity or experience. In actuality, the approach is apolitical and respects the various influences—including lineage—that have helped practitioners arrive exactly where they are.

Breaking Through to Training Secrets
Breaking Through *is a Love Letter to Karate* Kata *Bassai Dai* (拔塞)

Bassai Dai as an art form is practiced across a variety of systems. Variations of it can be found in Okinawan systems, Japanese Karate, Korean Tang Soo Do, traditional Taekwondo, and American Karate schools.

Its provenance, however, is lost in the mists of time.

Karate historians trace Bassai Dai *kata* to Okinawa in the late 18th Century, and from there its origins become patchy. My favorite martial arts author, Bruce D. Clayton, says Matsumura Sōkon, one of the original Karate masters of Okinawa, "is rumored to be the author of the Passai (Bassai) *kata*, but his love of secrecy makes this hard to prove" (Clayton 48).

How far back we want to locate its source material depends on the elasticity of our frame of reference. The similarities Bassai shares with Five Animals Kung Fu means we could connect-the-dots and reach all the way back to the 13th-century ("Animal Styles").

The *kanji* for Bassai (拔塞) is explained as "breaking through an enemy's fortress" ("Passai"), which is how I derived the title for this book. Bassai in its various incarnations is also known as Passai, Batsu-sai, or Balsek. Hanshi Clayton's book, *Shotokan's Secret: The Hidden Truth Behind Karate's Fighting Origins,* leads us to a profound revelation of Bassai. He believes Bassai's true meaning is "to pull out or to extract," postulating that the hidden purpose behind Bassai is its integral role in the security of the Okinawan royal family at the time ("Passai"). In other words, Bassai's hidden purpose may be to teach palace guards techniques and principles to combat enemy soldiers while extracting the royal family to safety.

As an instructor, the strategic clarity I gained from *Hanshi* Clayton and *Shotokan's Secret* resulted in a quantum leap in our applications training. The book breathed life into Bassai, irrespective of any of its various presumed meanings or its evolution across geopolitical lines.

▲ Bassai Dai, due to its practice in a variety of martial arts, is an ideal *kata* to illustrate how the JDK Method can be applied to *kata* in general to improve one's training and understanding in their chosen system.

While my journey with Bassai started a mere three decades ago, it is a legacy carried over from our Korean Karate roots. More than just another pattern for me to learn and teach, however, Bassai has been a passport to network and cross-train with practitioners from around the world and plumb its genetic structure across Okinawan, Japanese, American, and other combative styles.

Time and again, I return to this one form. I wonder what would drive a person to create a system like this. What kind of situations did he face? What skills did he have before this form? What was he trying to transmit to others with this lone *kata*?

Frankly, Bassai doesn't gain value because someone connects the dots back through several hundred years. Matsumura didn't intend for Bassai to be a reliquary. That he was the "chief martial arts instructor and bodyguard...to two Okinawan kings" meant he was pragmatic, tough, and ruthlessly effective ("Matsumura Sōkon"). I believe how this bodyguard would have us connect the dots paints a significantly different picture than the contrived videos on YouTube.

While Matsumura was secretive, he never denied that Bassai was his creation. That the *kata* has persisted over three centuries may indicate it wasn't meant to be sequestered. It was central to Matsumura's Karate's DNA, yet his pupils and progeny felt they needed to pay it forward to the rest of the world. From an unbroken line it thus landed upon us, prompting me to continue the search for relevance through the mists of time which have concealed it. I hope those that come after me will likewise take up the mantle and continue to pay it forward.

In our school, the foundation of any training is to become a tougher opponent. To do this we teach the student how to get "into the zone." Getting "into the zone," or achieving a flow state, is a "mental state… characterized by the complete absorption in what one does, and a resulting transformation in one's sense of time" ("Flow"). Getting into the zone helps us become more effective by reducing distractions and allowing us to function tactically under duress.

Traditional *dojo* etiquette, for instance, while often dismissed as irrelevant cultural appropriation, is an assortment of specific physical rituals which helps students and instructors ease into the "zone." Such physical rituals – from putting on the uniform, to bowing at the door, surveying the training area, adopting a particular posture, and practicing *kata* – sharpen one's mental focus.

Rituals, through constant mental visualization, along with the repetition of *kata* such as Bassai, develop a kind of mental construct for the practitioner. That is, the more one practices, the more one develops a distinct mnemonic device, a Mind Palace that enhances memory and recall (Blowers, 2018). While this mental space exists only in one's imagination, it is overlaid onto the blueprint of the practitioner's physical *dojo*. Simply willing it to happen, one can return whenever needed. The practitioner can visualize the training area, visualize various training partners, engage in training drills, or simply adopt that optimal mental state brought on within its familiar surrounds.

For example, I could be on the other side of the world, or in a business meeting, or experiencing some dreadful dental procedure. When I steeple my fingers or loosely put my right fist into my left palm, I enter my Mind Palace. I am physically present at the meeting or the dental procedure, but I am mentally back in the *dojo* with Bassai, filtering out extraneous, irrelevant stimuli. I'm linking to everything I've ever acquired from the form, surveying every skill I prize from its techniques, feeling the sinews of my muscles activate while I visualize its movements. I draw strength from this mentation that few non-practitioners could ever understand. Just that one hand formation, that *mudra*, is an indelible link to Bassai across time.

Breaking Through is a peek into our school's *mizong* (迷蹤), our "secret system." These are secret only because they are unique to how we train. People who've come to our school know we share these secrets without reservation. I share the secret applications in this book because they are pragmatic, within every student's power, and tap into the essence of hard style training. We readily share these because we all become better as we connect-the-dots with the right people.

This book reveals twelve applications inspired by Bassai Dai. Many of the applications come with variations and options within their sequencing. These are not more of the same form for solo practice. They prepare the practitioner's mind to eventually face an unscripted and dynamic situation.

We talk of our patterns as a syllabus, which may seem to indicate some grand scheme or neatly packaged solutions. However, *kata* is not a prepackaged fight plan. A *kata*'s 40-something movements will not develop fight IQ. I say it again: there is nothing to be gained if students don't deconstruct the *kata*, look for its true lessons, and drill the resulting lessons until those skills become second nature.

Allow me to speak directly to you once more.

As you study and practice the applications, I urge you not to compare them to how training "used to be." There is no single correct way to make adjustments according to the opponent which this method of training requires. You have to make initial assumptions, provide simple options, make more assumptions, and re-use existing skills whenever possible. And you will have to do this over and over and over again. Don't over think the techniques. Eventually, when faced with a dynamic opponent, you will know to let go of all else and clear the mind to be in the moment to read the opponent and to respond appropriately. This is a natural part of progression.

We don't believe that a single, correct formula exists for any application due to the fluid and dynamic nature of physical conflict. The applications in this book, like the sequences within them, do not adhere to a strict step-by-step formula. These applications are not traditional one-, two- or three-step exercises which feature prescribed defenses against prescribed attacks. Rather, the applications we present have been tested and trained countless times and proven to be an effective series of responses against the most common and likely exchanges, i.e. attacks and counterattacks.

Each application follows the paradigm of *if…then… else*. All start with a movement or technique inspired by Bassai Dai as a defense or response to an impending threat, such as a punch. The antagonist then responds to our defense, and we are forced to analyze their response and initiate a defense against the new attack, for which they again react to continue their attack. This exchange continues until the aggressor is unable to counter or press his attack. The lessons learned from training can then be re-used in future exchanges where they may continue to be found useful.

This is no longer Matsumura's Bassai. Through my lineage, its genetic structure has been passed along, gifted from one generation to the next. Seeing as how I've now received it as a gift, I have become one of its current custodians. And likewise, if you decide to receive it as a gift in your heart, you too may continue this lineage onwards. It is a great responsibility.

Shall we begin? ■

Bassai Dai

拔塞大

中道館

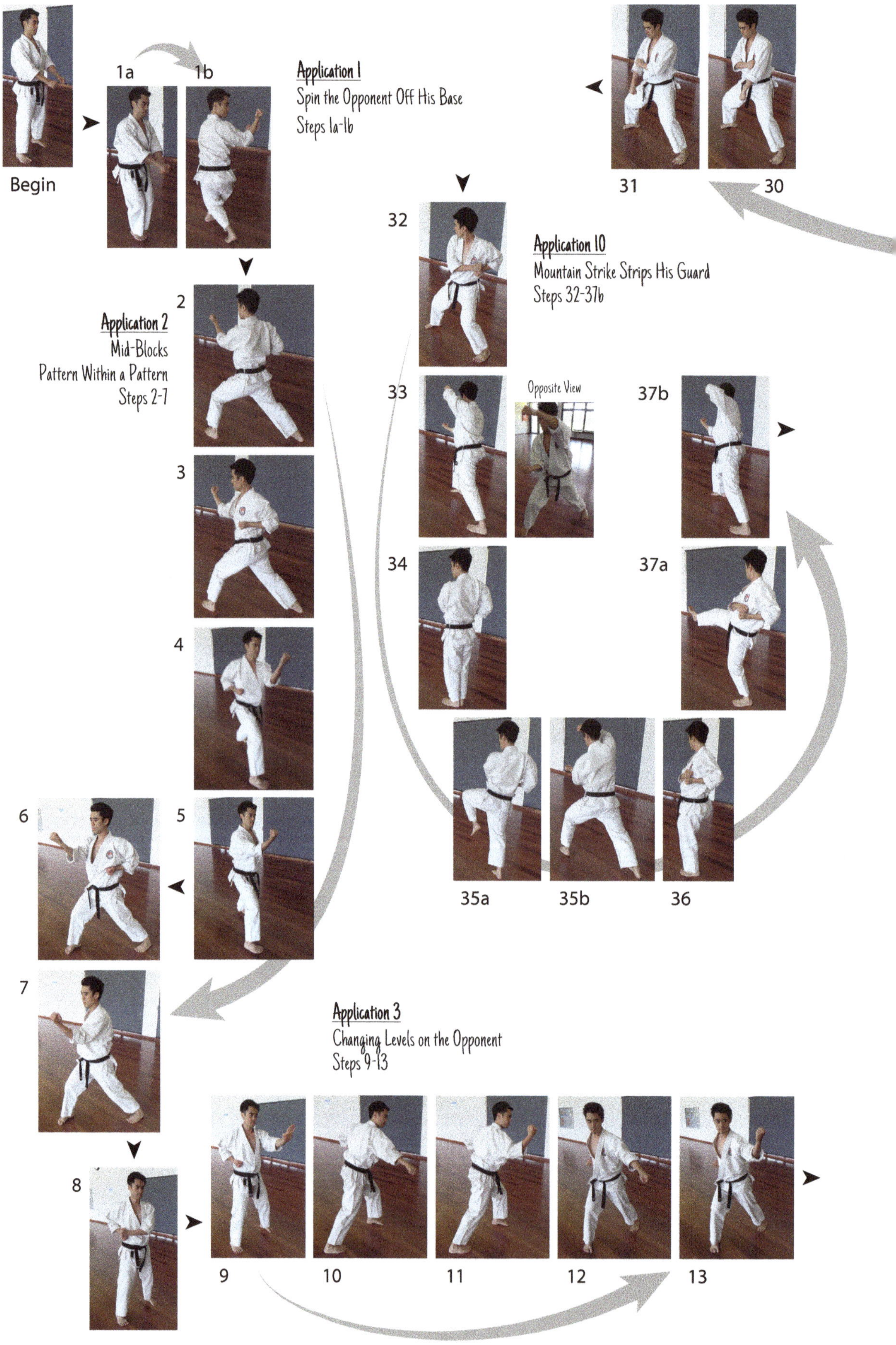

Begin
1a 1b

Application 1
Spin the Opponent Off His Base
Steps 1a-1b

Application 2
Mid-Blocks
Pattern Within a Pattern
Steps 2-7

2
3
4
5
6
7
8

Application 3
Changing Levels on the Opponent
Steps 9-13

9 10 11 12 13

Application 10
Mountain Strike Strips His Guard
Steps 32-37b

32
33 Opposite View 37b
34 37a
35a 35b 36

30 31

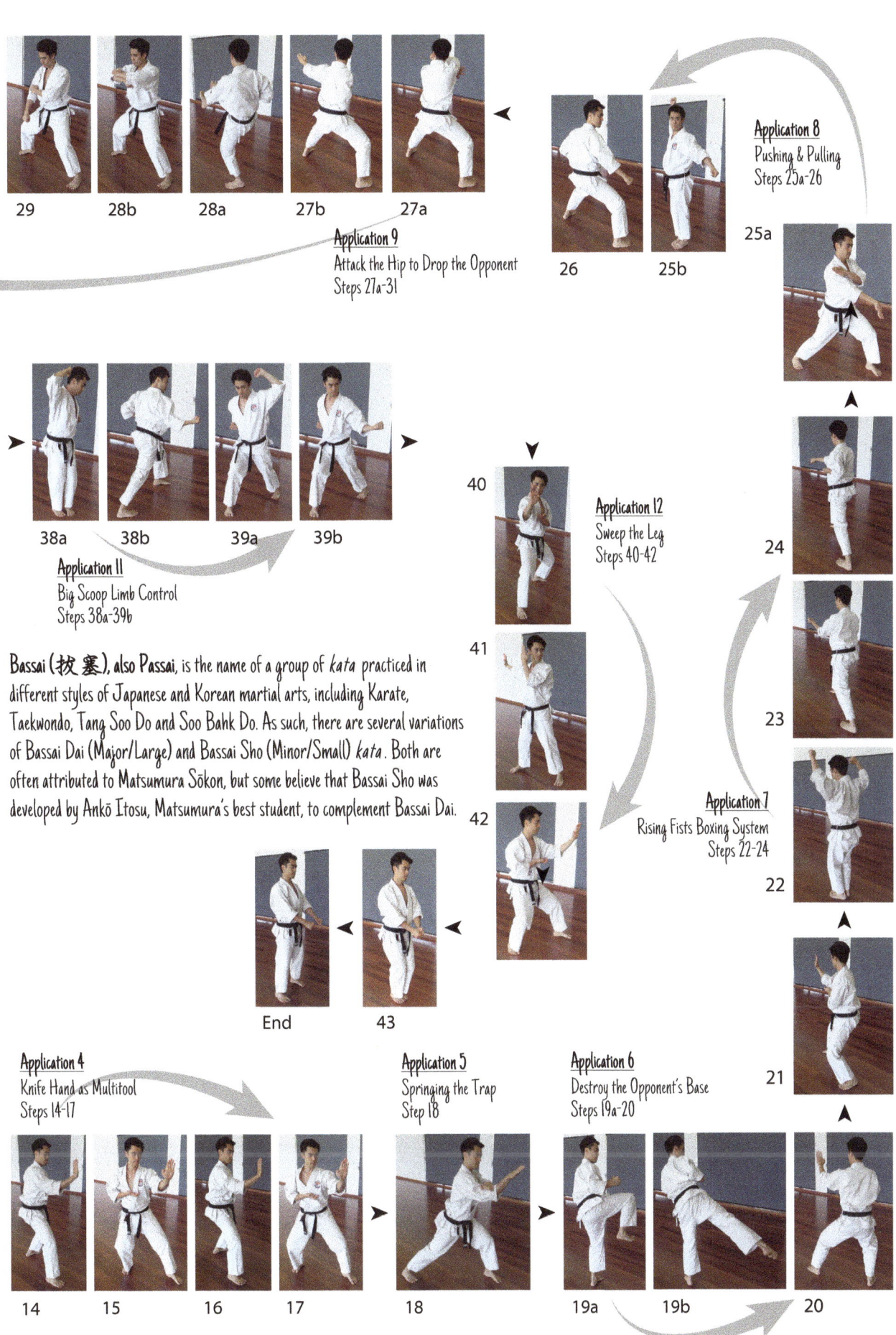

Bassai (拔塞), also Passai, is the name of a group of *kata* practiced in different styles of Japanese and Korean martial arts, including Karate, Taekwondo, Tang Soo Do and Soo Bahk Do. As such, there are several variations of Bassai Dai (Major/Large) and Bassai Sho (Minor/Small) *kata*. Both are often attributed to Matsumura Sōkon, but some believe that Bassai Sho was developed by Ankō Itosu, Matsumura's best student, to complement Bassai Dai.

Application 1

Application 1
Spin the Opponent Off His Base
Steps 1a-1b

1a Begin

1b

2

Application 2
Mid-Blocks
Pattern Within a Pattern
Steps 2-7

3

Spin the Opponent Off His Base
Application 1: Bassai Dai Steps 1a–1b

Our first application is extracted from the opening backfist/guarding block sequence from Step 1a and Step 1b of *Bassai Dai*, which we present as an aggressive neck manipulation takedown.

To access the opponent's neck, we need to bypass the raised guard and gap close, or deflect an oncoming attack and gap close, or work from a standing clinch.

There is no single way to engage an opponent. There is no single way a fight starts. Or ends.

The flight path of many traditional blocking techniques can be adapted to bypass a lead guard or a simple jab cross. Timed with a proper feint, some head movement and footwork, anyone with decent spatial awareness would have a fair chance to close the gap without eating too many oncoming strikes.

However we get through the opponent's raised guard, we must not chase his hands. If we slap his hand aside without trying to trap it to his body, his arm remains free, and he can retaliate immediately. In a combat situation, our opponent is not compelled to draw his hand back to his hip before punching us in the face!

In this application, we deflect the raised lead hand guard using an open palm slap and trap it, "listening" for a secondary attack. Traps like this not only guard against our opponent's combat tools but also link us to his structure, which offers additional kinesthetic benefits.

We "read" a shift in the opponent as an intent to attack with his second hand, so we immediately trap this secondary hand against his body as we close the distance between us. This ties up both of his weapons momentarily.

1.1.1 – Our opponent adopts an aggressive stance. We assume he is preparing to strike.

1.1.2 – We bypass the opponent's lead hand by deflecting his guard with an open palm slap.

1.1.3 – Our deflection traps the opponent's lead hand, which links to his structure and allows us to read his intention and prepare for a secondary offensive with our free hand.

and another well-timed strike or kick. Few traditional takedowns can be practiced without a gymnastics foam pit and all require maximum concentration to ensure partner safety.

While we seek to maintain safety in our training, a clean fall for a Judo tournament is far from the design of this application.

As our opponent drops to the floor, we follow through with a drop on the back of his head which meets the upward recoil of his bounce. This move with the help of gravity snaps the head forward and down into an unnatural and unpleasant landing, hyper flexing his neck.

Hyperflexion occurs when a joint is flexed beyond its maximum safe range of motion. Such extreme movement can result in life-long injuries to the opposing ligaments, tendons, and muscles.

Be likewise mindful of these dangers while training! ∎

1.1.12 – This illustration of "General Holding a Seal/Stamp" from the *Bubishi* shows a counter using a grab to the back of the head while lifting the chin, similar to Step 1b from *Bassai*.

Be aware and cautious when training! Injuries to the neck can be life altering — even deadly. They involve the bones and joints of the cervical spine (neck region), the intervertebral discs which act as shock absorbers between the bones of the spine, the muscles and ligaments that hold all these wonderful elements together, and the ever-important spinal cord ("Neck Injuries"). This application involves manipulating the opponent's head and neck, a dangerous proposition when one is careless. Sometimes, as in this application, we manipulate the head/neck as part of a larger, single component which allows us to likewise affect the opponent's balance. At other times, we manipulate the head/neck to purposefully cause damage to the opponent, as in hyperflexion. The slightest movement has potential to cause injury. **Practice extreme care when manipulating any part of the head/neck.**

Alternate Applications: General Holding a Seal/Stamp to Wrecking Ball for Multiple Opponents

An alternative to this spin takedown is a tactic featured in *The Bubishi* called "General Holding a Seal/Stamp" (Pic 1.1.12.) *The Bubishi* directs us to cross-step around the opponent's base and push his head straight up and back, ending with a hard connection to the floor (McCarthy 169). In this variation, the opponent-as-a-shield no longer applies. It gives us the opportunity to remove the opponent from the equation.

However, the off-balancing phenomenon from the opening moves of *Bassai Dai* affords us a unique advantage in a multiple opponent scenario.

As our opponent's cronies circle us, with our grip clamped down on our opponent's neck, prepared to drive his head to the ground, wouldn't some sort of weapon come in handy?

We need look no farther than what we already hold in our hands! The opponent teeters on his toes, trying to extricate himself from our grip and regain his balance. We, in contrast, hold in our hands an improvised 10-pound blunt-edged impact tool!

1.2.1 – The opponent on our right crosses the gap while the thug on our left scans for witnesses.

1.2.2 – We parry and roll around the attack...

1.2.3 – To slam a heel palm into the opponent's face/head...

1.2.4 – As we side step to increase our distance from the second thug and reach around to grasp behind the opponent's neck.

1.2.5 – We cross step and circle around the opponent and grasp his neck with our other hand to control and use him as a shield.

1.2.6 – We surge forward with a picture-perfect General Holding a Seal/Stamp to drive our opponent's head into the second thug.

Gripped in our hands, the opponent's skull becomes a wrecking ball that can be catapulted towards the opponent's back, *à la The Bubishi* (Pics 1.2.1–1.2.6), or swung laterally left and right (Pics 1.3.1–1.3.4).

Extrapolating from the General Holding a Seal/Stamp, the opponent's head becomes a rook on a chess board. And, like in chess, this is a major piece that can scythe left or right into circling opponents or sharpshoot a bad guy behind enemy lines.

Once the opponents collide, we can continue to use our held opponent as a shield and deal with the second thug, or simply capture another thug/shield.

Such fluidity in a multiple opponent scenario helps us mount a defensible retreat or advance towards a defensible location.

This tactic is ultra-pragmatic, so unpredictable, and so ruthlessly effective that even with control, I once accidentally TKO'd our school's two other black belts in a multiple opponent sparring scenario.

With a little experimentation, and employing skills already learned from basketball or other sports, we can wield this blunt-edged impact tool in such manner to make Matsumura proud. ■

1.3.1 – We've taken the initiative, but the second bad thug is on to it.

1.3.2 – We grip the opponent's neck and side step, wary of the thug circling to our left.

1.3.3 – We change direction and direct our intention towards the second thug.

1.3.4 – We drive our opponent's head laterally in a rising flight path directly into the second thug's face.

Questions for Self-Study
Prompts to Encourage Further Consideration

1. What flinch reactions or trained responses have you noticed from your training partners?

2. How can you take advantage of this knowledge in a physical encounter?

3. What is your favorite gap closing tactic?

Application 2
Mid-Blocks
Pattern Within a Pattern
Steps 2-7

2

3

4

5

6

Mid-Blocks Pattern Within a Pattern
Application 2: Bassai Dai Steps 2–7

This lesson and its drills are one of our favorite top-of-mind applications at JDK. Applications earn this favored status because they are easy to set up and repeatedly ask for simple, basic techniques which are trained thousands of times as beginning martial artists. When we have reached black belt and beyond, we have trained them hundreds of thousands of times, perhaps more.

Remember the story of that young black belt in a previous section? The one who depended on divine intervention if things didn't go his way? What are the chances he had an effective game plan going into that fight?

Well, his game plan had two parts. 1) Do the best he can to win. 2) If he is not winning, hope the divine intervenes on his behalf.

This is not an effective game plan, though most begin training and competing this way.

It lacks tactical understanding.

As we mature as martial artists, our understanding and training should mature as well. We should begin to develop game plans, aka strategies, designed to improve our training and its results. These game plans then become a syllabus for training.

A game plan optimizes a fighter's strengths against an opponent. The more we know of the opponent or the assumptions we can make of him, the better we can take advantage of lapses in his training and deficiencies in his skills. A focused game plan guides practice and helps train that winning edge.

That winning edge—in the hard style game plan—calls for a blitz attack strategy. This, we admit, has been an effective strategy since the beginning of time. It overwhelms the opponent's ability to identify and respond to a multitude of varying successive assaults.

Blitz attacks are the *modus operandi* of hard style practitioners, the purpose of all our line drills, chunking of sequences, speed drills, and dexterity exercises.

In this case, we blitz by closing the gap and ripping through attack sequences requiring little or no thought until our opponent's mental and physical sensibilities are overwhelmed and they are confused and overloaded, no longer able to defend against our onslaught.

Techniques: 3x Double Mid-Blocks

This application is the sequence of 3x double mid-blocks which launch Bassai (Pattern Diagram, Steps 2–7). This training exercise utilizes the blitz approach described above to explore gap closing on an opponent with his guard up to protect himself as he strikes.

There are three situational elements to consider in this application which determine the motions, direction and methods of our defense.

First, at which angle do we enter and make initial contact in a dynamic situation? As we turn or as our opponent circles us, an impending strike may come from multiple angles. It could come from outside our right side or our left side. Or inside of either arm. This happens because openings present themselves between and around our guard. If we use just the end point of a "traditional" blocking technique, we will never successfully deal with the opponent's oncoming attack.

The block is not the end point; it is the arc or path circumscribed by the motion of the block from its chamber to its end point. And the end point may not be the traditional end point trained in class. The end point of a technique reveals itself based on its purpose in any given encounter. That end point may fall short or extend beyond the traditional end point. Likewise, the preparatory movement may not be the full traditional chamber for the block. Together, these adaptations may be truncated or extended as to be nearly unrecognizable as a traditional technique.

Without the ability to foretell the direction of an attack, our defense in this scenario is to keep our arms moving left to right, and bounce them off the oncoming strikes at whatever point our arms make contact. It's a windshield wiper – not three separate pairs of mid-blocks but a continuous sequence of mid-blocks. Once we piece it together, this application is super easy to apply, pragmatic, and features a high probability of success.

Second, in relation to the opponent, where does the strike contact our lead hand? Is it from inside (Pic 2.1.1) or outside (Pic 2.2.1 or 2.3.1) of our lead arm? Trying to shut down the opponent's lead hand from either of these two positions requires different bypassing techniques. This is where the three pairs of middle blocks in Bassai elegantly address the scenario.

Third, how far away is our opponent? If our opponent is farther away, we must expand our "basic" technique's flight path. We reach towards the opponent by doing a "flyby" on his control tower. Or if the gap closes fast, we retract our arms closer around our head and upper body, creating a shell around us. As the distance ebbs and flows between opponent and defender, the form of the middle block is modified to match the distance between combatants and to find adherence to the opponent's structure. That is, the middle block on a line drill is a form and, like all forms, must be applied along a modified path for tactical advantage over the opponent. ∎

2.1.1 – We gap close, choosing to go to the inside of the opponent's lead guard, and move directly to his centerline.

2.1.2 – Our arm position allows for a cross draw to deflect the opponent's lead hand while providing cover against the opposite hand, or secondary tool.

2.1.3 – Our extended mid-block slams into the carotid artery on the opponent's neck before the opponent's secondary tool can find its target.

These first nine photos from the application (Pics 2.1.1–2.3.3) show different attempts to go around the opponent's lead guard.

These three sequences, or variations, have us working inside the lead guard (Pic 2.1.1,) hinging around the opponent's arm when our arms are crossed with the opponent's (Pic 2.2.1,) and moving outside of the opponent's guard (Pic 2.3.1).

This sounds like a lot of information, but it's necessary because our hands are held up in front of us and, as we move in relation to our opponent, different options—or opportunities—appear.

We're visually or kinesthetically registering the opponent's raised hand in three-dimensional space. We're folding the middle block around it to the inside or to the outside. The trapping with our rear hand works to slow the lead guard's counter, and the landing of the strike on his neck or side of his face is our prize. ∎

2.2.1 – In this variation to bypass the opponent's lead hand, we gap close and cross hands with our opponent for kinesthetic feedback.

2.2.2 – We relax our lead arm and slip forward to the opponent's centerline while chambering for an outward knifehand block and preparing to strike.

2.2.3 – Our legs drive us forward and generate power, which is then transmitted through our body structure as we hold him in place and launch a strike to his neck.

2.3.1 – At a stalemate, we read the situation, the environment, or our opponent's intentions via kinesthetic feedback and choose to go outside of the opponent's lead.

2.3.2 – We simultaneously close the gap; trap the opponent's lead hand with our rear, or secondary, hand; and raise our lead in preparation to strike.

2.3.3 – We strike our opponent's exposed neck, generating power from the contraction of our body and our linear movement into the opponent's center of mass.

The second part of this application (Pics 2.4.1–2.4.8 and 2.5.1–2.5.3) continues our blitz attack.

Once our forearm delivers its first payload, irrespective of it being a finishing strike, we have a much better chance of landing our rear cross (Pics 2.4.5–2.4.8).

At this point the opponent has been rocked with two strikes, and is trying to recover or regroup. As our rear hand makes contact, we continue the motion and manipulate his center of gravity by forcing his head backwards, applying pressure from the front (Pic 2.4.8).

2.4.1 – We prepare for our opponent's attack as before and choose our response.

2.4.2 – We bypass the lead, use footwork to close the distance, and unfurl our technique into the opponent's neck.

2.4.3 – Our striking hand cuts down on his lead, allowing us to move to the outside of his body and prepare for our next attack.

2.4.4 – As his lead hand clears our path of attack, our rear hand is poised to strike an opportune target.

2.4.5 – Our lead continues to snake into an underhook trap of the opponent's lead arm as our striking hand attacks his jaw or neck above his shoulder line.

2.4.6 – We follow through our attack to the opponent's head to thread our elbow to the centerline of his body.

For better control, we can come from around his neck and use a hair grab to pull him backwards to the floor (Pics 2.5.1–2.5.3). ∎

2.4.7 – We apply leverage using the side of our body and dropping our mass to force the opponent's center of gravity forward to the balls of his feet.

2.4.8 – We next right our posture and strike back towards his face, making him arch backward behind his center of gravity and topple to the ground.

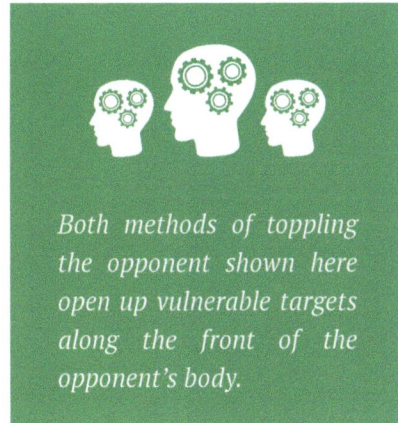

Both methods of toppling the opponent shown here open up vulnerable targets along the front of the opponent's body.

2.5.1 – Following through from our strike, we create the same leverage and force the opponent's center of gravity into place.

2.5.2 – Instead of backhanding his head, we perform a "comb over" and grab a fist full of his hair to control his head.

2.5.3 – This hair grab variation provides a stable purchase by which to pull him backwards to the floor.

This next group of photographs in this application (Pics 2.6.1–2.6.5 and 2.6.6–2.6.15) demonstrates what happens when our "windshield wiper" fails.

This sequence from the beginning of Bassai can be divided into two sequences which can stand alone or work together in tandem, as shown below.

In this scenario, our opposite hand strays outside our opponent's lead guard or primary attack (Pic 2.6.2). This may be because we had prepared to deflect a strike but guessed wrongly. Or our opponent might

2.6.1 – We prepare as before for our opponent's attack.

2.6.2 – But we find ourselves outside of his lead hand for any number of reasons.

2.6.3 – We use the chambering of the inside mid block to make connection and parry his lead hand as our rear hand prepares to trap the lead hand.

2.6.4 – We prepare to strike with our lead hand in a similar fashion as before. Our opponent feels pressure to respond to our raised hand.

2.6.5 – We complete the inside block and strike the side of the opponent's neck or collar bone, driving our center of gravity forward to crash into his body.

2.6.6 – The opponent attacks with his rear hand next. (From this point, the sequence may also be used as an application for a simple rear hand attack.)

have side-stepped and now our lead falls outside his guard. In either case, this creates an opening over our lead hand and shoulder which now offers our head as a target.

Our Plan B? We switch from using the middle block to the chamber of an outer forearm block (Pic 2.6.3; Pattern Diagram, Step 4). This chamber creates a shield against strikes sneaking through this hole in our defense.

2.6.7 – We counter using an outside mid block, which connects with and opens up the oncoming strike as our back hand prepares to deal with another strike.

2.6.8 – In this case, we only need deal with the opponent's single rear hand strike. We press it down while chambering our lead hand for the inside block (strike).

2.6.9 – Our inside block/hammerfist soundly attacks the backside of our opponent's neck.

2.6.10 – We continue our attack in harmony with Bassai and underhook the opponent's arm away from our body while preparing to launch an overhead strike/punch.

2.6.11 – We wedge/trap his arm as we land our strike/punch.

2.6.12 – We follow through to scoop his arm downward between our bodies and prepare our left hand for another mid block attack.

We then blitz a follow up using the folding and unfolding of the middle block directly from Bassai. We gap close and alternate plowing our forearms and hands into the opponent's upper body. We continue striking (Pics 2.6.4–2.6.13) until we can circle our opponent and take his head backwards, slamming him to the ground (Pics 2.6.14–2.6.15). ∎

2.6.13 – Our left hand rockets over his shoulder and connects with his jaw while our right continues to control his lead arm away from our body.

2.6.14 – We now scissor the opponent's right arm and drop our weight on his body, which pulls the opponent's center of gravity forward (between his knees).

2.6.15 – We release this pressure on the opponent by executing an outside block against his head to arch his body backwards and down to the floor.

In our final scenario for Application 2, our opponent's guard remains high and tight (Pic 2.7.1).

We swing our blocking arm under his elbow to strike his ribs. The impact causes him to flinch and drop his guard slightly. We trap his closest hand with our rear hand, drawing his focus (Pic 2.7.2).

Our large scooping swing brings our other arm high, from which we can either defend against a possible

2.7.1 – Our opponent anticipates an attack and erects a high and tight guard. We bring our left up to prepare to cover any strike to our face.

2.7.2 – We immediately guard his lead hand, drop into the pocket and strike laterally into his ribs or outer thigh. The sharp pain causes him to recoil and we trap his lead hand, drawing his focus.

2.7.3 – We continue the large circular motion of our strike which brings our arm high, a position from which to defend against a possible counter or launch a second strike.

2.7.4 – Our opponent fails to counter, so we drop our forearm to smash against his collarbone.

2.7.5 – Pain explodes into his shoulder and neck and down his arm. We follow through with a punch to the exposed jawline.

2.7.6 – All our punching practice from countless line drills finally pays dividends! Our fist connects with the opponent.

counter or launch another attack (Pic 2.7.3).

Since our opponent does not counter, we attack, bringing our forearm crashing down on his clavicle (Pic 2.7.4).

The middle block folding and unfolding blitz attack starts again until we've circled around to his side where we can once more influence his center of gravity and, using the motion of an outside block, disrupt his structure and drop him to the ground (Pics 2.7.5—2.7.8). ∎

2.7.7 – We follow through to shift his weight forward, lock his legs in place with our own, and weaken his structure (as in Pic 2.6.14).

2.7.8 – We release the pressure on our opponent with an outside block to his head, change his axis, and drop him outside his base (as in Pic 2.6.15).

Additional Principles

Recall the ease in both set up and the iteration of simple techniques. Look at how easy it is to modify our techniques on-the-fly to adapt to the reactions and movements of the opponent. We could use this application and then follow up with many of the other concepts presented throughout this book. Or with whatever other techniques come naturally from our own bag of tricks.

Note that we're not pulling our secondary tool to our hip. The *hikite* is a feature from line drills. Functionally, if we have latched onto an arm from the opponent, we can pull it to us, pin it against our body and immediately attack the joint. But if we are faced with an opponent who's trying to knock us out, both hands should be up in a guarding position, yet ready to strike.

It's logical to train so we can make split second decisions, especially under duress. Simple, effective tactics chunked together makes for intelligent training. As students, we have to break through the idea that complex, advanced, and standalone techniques are the measure of a martial artist. The truth is, as martial artists, we must break through to the understanding that, in reality, overly complex, standalone, advanced techniques make for poor training. Under duress, in a fluid combat situation, such techniques are difficult to perform and, therefore, much less effective. ∎

Questions for Self-Study
Prompts to Encourage Further Consideration

1. What are your favorite combinations?

2. How do you vary those combinations when you train? How often do you train them?

3. If you were creating a pattern, how would you embed those combos within it?

Application 3

35a

Application 3
Changing Levels on the Opponent
Steps 9-13

9

10

11

12

Changing Levels on the Opponent
Application 3: Bassai Dai Steps 9–13

Combative sport rules, duty of care and safety policies may be the biggest reasons why martial arts have gained widespread popularity and at the same time been watered down over the last 60 years.

Competition scenarios and formats were designed for safe exchanges. Strikes are thrown but never land, certain areas in the body are designated "no go" zones to avoid injuries, and practitioners of striking arts—such as Tae Kwon Do—must avoid clinching, wrestling, or throwing opponents due to the aforementioned sporting rules. Competitors—now often called "players" not fighters—are also separated by weight class and belt rank to further create an atmosphere of equality among them.

This is a large generalization, of course. There are exceptions. Some Karate tournaments still allow throws, takedowns and a finishing strike which follows. Yet organizers of all martial arts sporting events, regardless of art or format, by definition must develop and enforce rules to ensure the safety of competitors and a sense of fair play for all.

Unfortunately, we do not have the luxury of safety and fair play against a real opponent in a self-defense situation.

In a martial arts class, our instructor might show us a striking technique, and we then get to power it into a target. It's not like there's no benefit from interpreting all techniques from *kata* as a strike or kick and drilling them like this into a power shield. It's great for kinetic chaining, for cardio, and even for mental health.

But the reality is: *No one's going to give us a free shot*.

Simply believing we can deliver strikes without encountering a raised guard or resistance of some sort does not make that belief a reality.

◄ A dynamic encounter against a real opponent (or opponents) requires skills which are not developed while training for competition. Outside the arena, there are no rules to govern engagement. A street-wise aggressor hits back in ways far different than an opponent in a martial art class or competitive match. He may also use a concealed weapon (or weapons), or improvise nearby objects as weapons, and bring multiple opponents into the fray against us, a lone adversary. Not to mention emotional and auditory distractions, such as a heated verbal exchange or the cheers or goading of bystanders.

The application we posit here takes advantage of misdirection and our opponent's flinch response to work around his guard.

This application starts with brush-draws of an oncoming strike and a preemptive reach towards the opponent's face. This invades his centerline awareness, engages him at head level, and is likely to cause him to raise his guard high and tight.

Brush-draw might be an unfamiliar term. After making a connection with the opponent's arm, instead of laterally moving it aside, we "suck" the limb towards our body and off to the side. It's done lightly, like we're brushing the opponent's arm as we draw it just slightly off the edge of our body. The brush-draw is

3.1.1 – We square up with our opponent. His stance mirrors our own. His guard is high and tight.

3.1.2 – We extend our lead hand toward our opponent's eyes to occupy his centerline focus.

3.1.3 – As soon as we obstruct his view, we drop into the pocket and strike his nearest iliac crest, rocking his weight to his rear foot.

3.1.4 – Immediately, we raise our body and fire a strike from his hip to his protruding jawline or the side of his neck. Notice that we continue to trap his right arm.

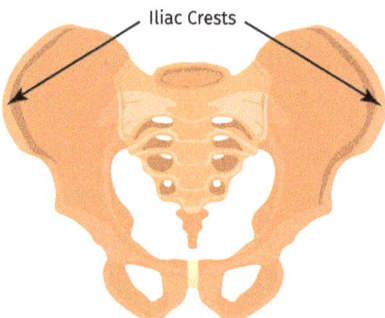

3.1.5 – Striking an iliac crest of the pubic bone causes our opponent's structure to turn and/or partially fold, pulling his head forward and down.

possible because the opponent subconsciously resists the connection between us.

Once the opponent's guard is high, we drop our head level and punch downward to his closest iliac crest—the outer-most flanges on each side of the pelvic bone (Pic 3.1.5)—causing our opponent's hip to shift backwards and head to jut forward (Pics 3.1.3 and 3.2.3).

Part of this response is an involuntary reaction to protect his pelvic region.

Our follow up "mid-block" then rises up and greets his protruding jaw or the side of his neck. Or, as Pic 3.1.4 suggests, his jawline can be targeted with an upward inverted fore-knuckle strike, otherwise known as an uppercut.

3.2.1 – We square off against our opponent, but this time his stance is opposite of our own.

3.2.2 – We once more occupy his visual field and tuck our head tighter to guard against a secondary attack.

3.2.3 – We strike his nearest iliac crest, dropping our bodyweight into the technique. Our opposite hand presses against his lead arm to apply pressure to his system.

3.2.4 – We could punch from under the opponent's arm, but instead we clear his lead arm and tension his wrist, then fire an inverted upset punch to his jaw.

We can follow through—crashing our body against the joint of his arm or lunging forward to drive our knee into the leg which supports most of his body weight. These tactics exactly follow the next movement (Step 14) of the pattern.

Important Observations

From the opponent's perspective, our downward punch and body drop makes our head disappear from view. The impact on his iliac crest doesn't seem altogether threatening, but it disorients and sets him up for some comeuppance.

This application is a huge departure from line drill exercises. We can try this tactic whenever there's a significant height difference, or when the opponent only focuses on targeting head level strikes. This kind of opponent may get locked into a sort of tunnel vision. So, when we level change, this drops us out of view or the anticipated reach of his arms and gives us a tactical—albeit momentary—advantage.

Using bodyweight to accelerate the strike and dropping to a lower level is what boxers describe as "working in the pocket." The opponent who is over-reaching or has raised a high and tight guard will not be prepared for such a change in level and the strike. He will need time to adapt his tactics and re-engage at this lower level.

Unlike a boxer's punch, this strike is not done with shoulder rotation. Neither is it done with hip rotation as with a reverse snap punch. This lowered strike, similar to centerline punches, requires a vertical cycling of your shoulder to complement the downward movement of bodyweight. It is somewhat similar to the "Sine Wave" practiced by the International Taekwon-Do Federation (or ITF)—an up-down motion of the body believed to increase the power of a strike, such as a punch.

The Sine Wave method is portrayed as being a new and scientific way of generating power ("Taekwondo Sine Wave"). In essence, the move is about supporting any strike with a corresponding drop into a stance. The Sine Wave concept has practitioners raising themselves and then dropping into various techniques many times throughout their forms. While it is not without criticism, the up-down motion of the Sine Wave has tactical value yet to be fully explored.

Our punch to the iliac crest is analogous to the Sine Wave movement as it goes into the trough or valley of its wave. The strike to the hip is fired in a downward cycling motion like a train's steam cylinder turning its leading drive wheel. As we finish the downward cycle, our hand continues back towards our body and starts to cycle upward.

Which brings our weapon back into play. When it finally makes contact, it's driven upwards by our legs and posterior chain muscles.

Working "in the pocket" confounds those anticipating a slugfest at mid- or close range. We must be careful when we drop levels to keep lateral exits open. We must also beware of those opponents who can switch their game plan and swarm us or sprawl us to the ground.

If the opponent registers our drop of level and attempts to adapt, we can choose to connect with a headbutt, a shoulder roll or, as this application presents, any part of the fist or forearm. We have to insinuate between the opponent's limbs and materialize whatever technique on the fly. These strikes are for heat-seeking loopholes in three-dimensional space (Pic 3.1.4). We must develop the ability to bait the opponent and identify these openings.

We should also be practicing footwork that allows oblique moves to the sides, laterally away from the opponent's centerline, and we must be accustomed to switching directions at close range.

Working this application—and the others in this book—using the JDK Method helps us to practice these additional skills that are less apparent. ∎

Questions for Self-Study
Prompts for Further Consideration & Training

1. Any traditional technique that requires you to raise your arm should be re-examined for when you come up from working in "the pocket." How far up do you need to reach?

2. How do you protect your head when you drop levels?

3. How does the OODA Loop apply in scenarios such as this?

As we have begun to see—via the applications presented herein—a block fulfills many distinct and various functions such as traps, deflections, coverage, or parries.

The "no real block" statement might paraphrase something Bruce Lee once said: "A block is more than a block."

Our block—or "reception" of the opponent's initiative—depends on how nice we feel at that moment. We can choose to "receive" the opponent's initiative softly—or we can choose to receive it not-so-softly. If the opponent is so deserving, we can transmit our full body weight through a limb into the his structure.

These elements become clearer as we practice this application (Pics 4.1.1–4.1.6).

The knife hand movement can be applied to a jab-cross combo to deflect the arm from the outside as easily as from the inside (Pic 4.1.2). The chambering of the knife hand allows both arms to intercept the oncoming limb, guiding its trajectory from our centerline. If one hand fails to deflect the strike, the other acts as its backup.

We want to be as proactive as possible as we meet the oncoming strike. Deflecting the opponent's strike early means it's not yet traveling as fast as it will be when it nears us. We do this by reaching out with our technique. If, however, we are not able to visually see or feel the oncoming tool or we are not in a position to reach forward, then the deflection or cover needs to happen closer to our body.

To elicit pain, we choose to meet the ungloved strike directly with the blade of our forearm (Pic 4.1.2). Our chambering hand acts as a catcher's mitt and guides the strike toward the hard edge of our forearm. This use of the forearm as "immovable armor" is an important concept for traditional techniques. Once we deflect the

4.1.4 – We tap the secondary strike with same hand and lift the arm. This covers the side of our head and readies us for possible counters, as our knife hand strike finds his exposed neck all too efficiently.

4.1.5 – We gap close, spin our body, and use that motion to drive the rising elbow from our left hand into his jawline.

4.1.6 – We shift our body into his space, flexing his head backwards (as we did in Application 2). This unbalancing can accelerate him into a nearby structure or transform him into a battering ram against other combatants.

limb, we shift to move inside or outside of the opponent's strike.

As the shock goes into his lead jab, we turn obliquely and direct ourselves toward his opposite shoulder (Pic 4.1.3)—temporarily eliminating our head as a target. This movement drives us toward his secondary tool. Our hand that's already up acts as a cover for our face. Our new lead arm proactively reaches forward and brush-draws the oncoming cross (see page 48 for more information about brush-draw).

This wipe-on-wipe-off movement forms a planar surface—we're slicing the outside curve of his strike, surfing that trajectory of his arm, and creating invisible armor with the flight path of our technique. If his cross is yet to launch, we surge more with our feet to jam or shut down his limb.

As important as waving our hands around, our footwork has us circling the opponent to deal with incoming strikes. This is a skill not fully appreciated in a line drill environment.

When we are in a large class, we practice individual techniques or combinations in nice even, straight lines. We start from one end of the room and proceed to the other while making the movements. These line drills are forms and, like all forms, we must learn to use—or apply—them

Are we gap closing, engaged in melee exchange, or displacing the opponent's center of gravity? If we are gap closing, we direct our line drill towards the opponent. However, as we search for tactical advantage, sometimes our forward drive needs to obliquely pass or circle the opponent—which is what we're doing in Pic 4.1.3. We direct our body to the outside of his shoulder and our arms act like a wind vane because that gives us tactical advantage.

How far we steer ourselves toward the shoulder and then toward his strike depends on how wide he swings that arm. The more linear his strike, the tighter our path. To get there, we tighten our core, exhale, drop our bodyweight and drive the legs so we are skimming the orbit of our opponent's strike (Pic 4.1.4). As we pass his strike tangentially, we'll be in a position to strike from where he has no cover—while he struggles to regroup.

If we aren't in a position to control or take down the opponent, then we have no choice but to loosen him up. We do this by raising our arm forward in a chamber and connecting with a proactive elbow. Then dropping and accelerating our knife hand, connecting with the blade of the hand. The knife hand, blade of the forearm, or the elbow—they are a continuum of the same weapon, all connected to our structure and linked to our center of gravity. We choose how to deliver the knife hand based on how the angle of entry appears.

A Note About Footwork

In a close quarter scenario, we have to stutter-step to nudge ourselves around the circle, work with the straddle stance to strafe laterally, and use instances of cross steps or on-the-spot turns—all of which give us the ability to circle a particular target.

Frequently used in sports, a stutter-step occurs when—using small, quick steps—we make sudden stops and starts to deceive or evade an opponent ("Definition of 'stutter-step'").

It's harder for the opponent to land his strike at close range while we're moving like this. The turn of our body, the shift forward, and our arm movement makes it difficult to track lateral movement. The opponent eventually leaves his entire side wide open, finds it hard to retract or repurpose his limb, or gets his body jammed, and then...check mate. ■

Questions for Self-Study
Prompts for Further Consideration & Training

1. Switching directions and circling the opponent are tactically advantageous. If so, what are techniques you would use in tandem with such movement?

2. Do you move before the opponent's strike? During the strike? Or after the strike?

Application 5

43

Application 5
Springing the Trap
Step 18

Application 6
Destroy the Opp
Steps 19a-20

17

18

19a

Springing the Trap
Application 5: Bassai Dai Step 18

As described previously, guidelines which support safe competition dictate many details of daily training in various martial arts. That is to say, "fists of fury" entertain an audience, and some competitions actively discourage tactics which slow down exchanges between opponents. The increased flurry of approved combat techniques helps maintain audience interest and, thus, combative sports continue to flourish.

In a dynamic, always-changing situation, however, there's no telling what the opponent might do.

Our opponent in this scenario has bridged the gap, trapped our arm and seeks to control our structure (Pic 5.1.2). Having our lead guard jammed means we can't use it momentarily. The trap distracts our focus and, since it minimizes how we might respond, frustrates us. The kinesthetic connection also allows our opponent to read our next move with greater accuracy. Experience on his part might also predict a typical response from a typical opponent. This reasoning leads us to assume a real opponent will likely jam our primary weapon, our free hand.

A sound strategy, then, would be to train a counter for when our opponent traps our lead hand and anticipates that we'll strike with our free hand.

A Word About Traps

I was initially taught this crossing of hands as a Figure 4 Wrist Lock. Standalone wrist locks are a great skill to have and we teach them at Joong Do Kwan, but to a hard stylist they're less important than standing clinch skills, shoulder locks, arm bars, takedowns, or throws. As a result, Joong Do Kwan prioritizes this application instead of a wrist lock as just one counter to an arm trap—a way out from a position of disadvantage.

A trap locks the extremity onto the structure. The arm isn't just slapped to one side or pushed downwards to the ground. If the arm is merely deflected instead of trapped, it's simple enough to draw the arm back and piston it forward again. Or if our arm gets struck or "blocked" hard, we could go with the energy and bring our secondary tool into play. A good trap, however, locks our weapon between our body mass and the opponent's body mass. In a split second, while we struggle to release our arm, we're eating an attack to our face.

A trap isn't a specific technique. We don't see it overtly practiced in forms. In fact, I would say many techniques in *kata* could be used to trap an arm or limb. A simple hand extension would do the job. "Zooming with our feet" so our shoulder presses against the opponent's arm would also work.

If I were to design a *kata* to avoid most young practitioners' belief that all techniques in *kata* are simply strikes, I would include trapping skills into the design by one or all of the following:

1. a forward movement of the body with a retreating arm technique (Pattern Diagram, Step 19a, which shows a knife hand morphing into a double gripping technique before the side kick);
2. a backward movement of the body with an extension of the arm (Pattern Diagram, Step 17, in which a knife hand is extended as the leg is withdrawn); or
3. a rotation and drawing of the extended hand towards one side (Pattern Diagram, Step 8,

5.1.1 – The opponent closes and we raise our hands.

5.1.2 – Our opponent traps our lead guard with his right hand.

5.1.3 – We feel the trap and draw him to commit by rotating our body in place. The trapped side pulls back while our free hand reaches for his eyes.

5.1.4 – Our free hand circles over the trapping hand—covering against any secondary strike before we encircle his trapping arm.

5.1.5 – We hook our fingers over our upper elbow and, closing the gap, roll our arms to fold his hand to the front of his shoulder, directing force horizontally into his body.

5.1.6 – Once he falls for our forward ruse and begins to resist, we leverage his hand up over his shoulder, redirecting force downward into his shoulder.

5.1.7 – We pivot our locked arms outside the opponent's base to complete our circle, toppling him.

5.1.8 – Once our opponent is downed, we can drop a knee on him with impunity.

when we pull the extended middle block to our side as we turn to the front).

I could list examples where traps may be found within the *kata* practiced within our system. The fact remains—control of an opponent's limbs isn't accomplished by any single technique. We trap by reading the interplay of distance in an engagement, and the opponent's skeletal structure. It's our footwork, close quarter skills, and acquired sensitivity that leads to tactical advantage. Ongoing partner work—including the applications in this book—helps us refine these skills.

In this application, our particular counter to the opponent's trap looks like some graceful dance.

As we raise our lead hand as cover, we feel the pressure of the trap on our arm (Pic 5.1.2). We absorb this forward pressure by rotating our body in place and pulling back from the trap. We've made no move to overtly gap close, but we have maintained our balance and are now within reach of him.

As the opponent reads the "pulling away" of our body, he may increase the forward pressure of his trap by extending his reach or leaning forward into his technique, though we've not actually changed our distance.

Next, we reach forward with our rear hand to obscure his visual field and trigger a flinch response from him (Pic 5.1.3). In his mind, the hand in his face threatens to connect with his eyes, so he acts reflexively. Our extended hand also runs interference against his secondary tool if need be.

As our opponent gauges his predicament, we draw the extended arm back and across his trapping arm (Pic 5.1.4). If he pulls away or pushes into us, we read this and go with his movement. We interweave our arms with his, hooking our lower hand over our opposite elbow, scissoring his arm and linking him to our center of gravity (Pic 5.1.5). We call this a Figure 4 Lock in our system.

To stay in this arms-crossed position would give him the opportunity to target our face with his free hand. We move our head towards his shoulder, continue the snaking movement of the Figure 4 Lock, and drive forward toward his body. These movements increase the tension on his wrist, elbow, and shoulder joint. At this point our opponent will recognize that we're driving forward into his body, so he "digs in" to counteract our forward motion.

The opponent may be distracted by the mounting pain in his arm. However, there's no desperation yet as the pressure is mostly in front of his chest. He's in fact still able to counter our forward drive with his legs and retains control of his balance—at least for the time being (Pic 5.1.5)!

We maintain this constant head-on pressure and then suddenly swing it on a vertical axis to the top of his shoulder (Pic 5.1.6). This immediately changes the forward pressure from his chest into a downward pressure through the top of his shoulder and into his base. The move flexes his shoulder backwards and disrupts his underlying structure. With the sudden flexion and rotation of the shoulder, he cannot adapt fast enough to relieve the pressure or maintain his balance any longer.

Attacking the shoulder joint like this allows us to flat spin him off his base (Pic 5.1.7). This means we aim for a point outside his base and pull him horizontally in a circular but ever-tightening orbit. As his shoulder level drops toward the ground outside his base, the nature of his landing is entirely up to us (Pic 5.1.8). His only recourse is divine intervention.

This exact same application works with either arm trying to trap us, as demonstrated in the next group of photos (Pics 5.2.1–5.2.7). ∎

5.2.1 – The opponent closes and we instinctively raise our hands.

5.2.2 – Our opponent traps our lead guard (this time with his left hand).

5.2.3 – We rotate our body in place, which draws him forward to close the gap. This over extends him as we immediately take his vision with our free hand.

5.2.4 – The opponent reacts to our ruse and we brush-draw his trapping arm, encircling his arm and hooking our fingers over our opposite elbow in a Figure 4 Lock.

5.2.5 – We negate attempts to pull his arm away using footwork while applying pressure to the front of his shoulder. Next, we shift the vector of force from his chest to the top of his shoulder.

5.2.6 – We kinesthetically feel his center of gravity move to the edge of his base to relieve the pressure of our lock, so we pivot to direct his shoulder outside his base and to the floor.

5.2.7 – Our opponent succumbs to our counter.

We choose how our opponent falls. We can allow him to land gently, or we can accelerate his head and body into the floor. We might also drop a knee on him after as well if warranted.

Questions for Self-Study
Prompts for Further Consideration & Training

1. As we apply a trap, what else would we do that might slow the opponent and hide our intentions?

2. How do you prefer to cover yourself against a secondary attack when your lead arm is trapped or jammed?

Application 6
Destroy the Opponent's Base
Steps 19a-20

Destroy the Opponent's Base

Application 6: Bassai Dai Steps 19a–20

Turns & Takedowns in *Kata*

There are numerous mainstream thoughts on how to interpret technique sequences from *kata*.

One such idea looks at the turns in the form. A turn in the form is said to signify we've taken down the opponent, he's out for the count, and we turn to face another combatant.

Another way of interpreting a turn in *kata* says that we've engaged the opponent, gone into a clinch and have thrown him using our body as a pivot point. The turn itself is the throw.

These ideas are not without merit. However, anyone with a working knowledge of takedowns knows that *forms don't teach us how or when to throw*. We learn how to throw by throwing. The throw occurs when it occurs, not when the form thinks it should. In fact, we don't even have to use our body as a pivot to drop an opponent.

We should turn all the time in combat. Turns can be partial turns or full turns as we move to find a better angle of engagement with the opponent. Or to place that opponent between us and other combatants so we can keep them clearly in view in front of us or to manage space so we can nullify a strike with body positioning.

Shuhari & Bassai Dai *Kata*

The takedowns illustrated in this application are a departure from the standard interpretation of Bassai Dai *kata*. They are one of the lessons taught to us by Bassai when we leave the form (see *Shuhari*, page 16).

6.1.1 – The opponent squares up but doesn't give anything away.

6.1.2 – We take the initiative and double-tap his lead hand and press it to clear it.

6.1.3 – As in other applications we shoot our hand towards the opponent's face to distract him, and he either flinches or moves to clear his line of sight.

In fact, all the applications presented in *Breaking Through* are lessons taught by the form as we explored its prescribed movements and their explicit lessons and moved beyond them.

This application reminds us that we don't win fights by playing a defense-only game. We're developing this side kick as only one of "a very particular set of skills" to inflict maximum damage.

6.1.4 – We latch onto the opponent's lead arm and flex our elbows forward, which turns his body to the side. He may try a counter strike but our limbs help shield us.

6.1.5 – The opponent's lead leg is now vulnerable to the huge lateral swing of our chambering knee, which lifts the leg and destroys that support.

6.1.6 – As his lead leg clears the floor, we unleash a side kick to his remaining leg, which crumples his remaining support.

6.1.7 – The opponent's foundation weakened, we reach for his neck.

6.1.8 – We latch onto his structure and apply force to his head. This contorts his body outside his base and destabilizes him.

6.1.9 – We continue to read his structural balance and make adjustments so his axis tilts back behind his base.

General Application

Application 6 has two parts:

1. Knee the opponent's closest leg and then kick his supporting leg (Pics 6.1.1–6.1.6);
2. Take the opponent's head and topple him into the ground (Pics 6.1.7–6.1.10).

As we square up against our opponent, we bring our guard up high and seek to occupy his upper gate (Pic 6.1.1). We move to his centerline and trap his lead hand, protecting that opening (Pic 6.1.2). The surge to his face causes him to recoil and contemplate a counter (Pic 6.1.3). To complete the misdirection, we go for an arm control by latching onto his lower and upper forearm (Pic 6.1.4).

Once our feint is sold, we go low. Our chamber for the side kick acts as a battering ram (Pic 6.1.5). It connects to sensitive areas inside or outside of his thigh. This knee-kick is as indiscriminate as it is effective; we can use the tactic on either leg (as shown in Pics 6.2.1–6.2.10).

Striking our opponent's leg with this movement scythes it up and off the ground, causing him to lurch almost a full 90 degrees. He only keeps his balance by trying to land on his struck leg and straightening his opposite leg (Pics 6.1.5–6.1.6).

Our next move aims all the potential energy from our chambered side kick into the side of the supporting knee that now solely supports the opponent (Pic 6.1.6). Our kick lands unimpeded, destroying the joint or, in the extreme, results in loss of the limb. The fully extended side kick, as found in Bassai, is a devastating strike anywhere it connects.

A turn and a knife hand block occur at this point in Bassai (Pattern Diagram, Step 20). For these movements, we choose to go for a takedown because we have already taken our opponent's support structure, unless of course we have another tactical need to use him as a shield.

After the side kick to the opponent's supporting knee, we connect with his skeletal structure by placing a hand on his neck (Pic 6.1.6), read the status of his

6.1.10 – He topples to the floor close to our feet, grateful to not have been pitched headfirst into the floorboards.

◄ **Train with great care!** Attacking the knee, even during training, is a serious consideration. We summarize Dr. Stefan Erikkson from *Fight Times*: Injury to the joint can lead to permanent loss of mobility and, in the extreme, loss of the leg. Even minimal force such as simple twisting can injure the ligaments which make up the joint. Only 80-100 pounds of external force can dislocate the average knee. A laterally directed kick of sufficient force to the inside or outside of the knee results in a much more serious injury — potentially limb threatening. *The leg does not need to be fully extended in order to be injured laterally* (italicized for emphasis).

6.2.1 – We square off against our opponent once more, only this time he attacks with his right.

6.2.2 – We cross over and double tap his lead arm as we did in the first series of photographs.

6.2.3 – We reach forward, driving the blade of our forearm into his clavicle and hooking his lead arm.

6.2.4 – We flex out our elbows as before and latch onto his arm. We look away from his secondary tool to find the targets for our kick.

6.2.5 – The huge chamber for our side kick—using our knee or the top of our shin—impacts the inside of our opponent's thigh.

6.2.6 – As the force of our chamber lifts his leg into the air, we align our side kick with his only remaining support structure.

6.2.7 – Our side kick connects with the inside of his knee, making it hard—perhaps impossible—for him to stand.

6.2.8 – As the *kata* dictates, we latch our hand around his head to connect to his structure and read his balance.

With our hand connected to the opponent's structure at his neck, we can take him down, make him a shield or turn him into a battering ram—aka a Wrecking Ball against other combatants (see Application 1).

balance, and use his head to shift him out of his base (Pic 6.1.7). Once he's past the tipping point, we compress his lopsided structure towards the floor, moving his head into the void as we slip out of the way (Pics 6.1.8–6.1.10).

As shown in the second series of photos (Pics 6.2.1–6.2.10), this application applies just as well if the opponent attacks with the opposite hand, requiring only a few minor adjustments.

The takedown in this application clearly departs from the standard interpretation of Bassai Dai. Although the takedown was once obligatory as the indicator of a successful *bunkai*, it is now moot for our training at JDK. We have strayed farther from the *kata* and learned additional lessons—inspired by the *kata* but not limited to its sequence of techniques.

Explaining the Void

The void is an important concept in takedowns taught at the JDK. I have trained hard stylists who are unfamiliar with the void or how to recognize it on the ground and, therefore, can't effectively execute takedowns.

Many years ago, looking through a Judo manual, I saw a stance diagram with arrows that showed where a *judoka* is strong—and where a *judoka* is weak and can be easily toppled.

Some years later at a seminar, the late *Soke* Don Angier, an Aikijujutsu master, illustrated the same concept but in a slightly different way. He drew an imaginary line between the feet to create the base of a triangle and noted that the apex of that triangle (the highest point opposite its base) is the space where the opponent can be thrown. The void is that apex—that spot on the floor—where the person falls (Pic 6.2.11–6.2.14).

Grasping the concept of the void requires an understanding of one's own body mechanics and the opponent's structure, as well as the flight path a takedown should follow in three-dimensional space to take advantage of the void.

The opponent's flight path doesn't need to be a direct beeline for the void. Some takedowns require pushing and pulling and then maybe a circular pathway. Especially if we want to reduce the risk of injury to the opponent by landing him gently.

6.2.9 – In this instance, we choose to spin him around on his base, step aside, and drop him into the void to the floor.

6.2.10 – Our opponent seems to have fallen and can't get up.

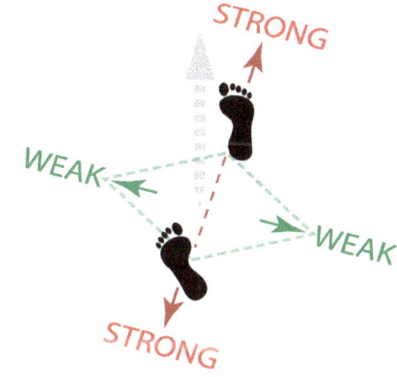

6.2.11 – A diagram of the void, showing where an opponent is weak and can be toppled.

The void is related to *chi* in some regards. At the JDK, we think of the void as an extension of how *chi* works. *Chi* flows through the body and can be directed. Thus, *chi* is a training aid to coordinate the necessary body dynamics and mechanics.

The void provides a destination and orchestrates the process of disrupting the opponent's balance, structure and his place in three-dimensional space. Rather than provide step-by-step, one-size-fits-all instructions, the JDK Method asks students to start the technique, read the opponent's flow, then aim his entire body into the void. The individual processes in the takedown simply follow suit.

We learn how to best start the technique, how to read the opponent's flow and how to aim the opponent's body at the void as we practice takedowns with our partners. We each learn in our own way with our own unique gifts and limitations and, then, how we, as a unique individual, can best accomplish tossing opponents into the void.

At any time during a takedown, we can assess whether or not we're going to throw our opponent gently or throw him roughly. We can interrupt the flow and redirect it. Even in mid-air we can change the way the opponent lands. Or we can stop a part of his body from following the flight path—while the rest of his body continues unimpeded. Gravity tears the limb for us. And gravity, not muscular force, creates the impact when our opponent finds the void. ∎

6.2.12 – A diagram of the void, placed atop a sequence of photos to illustrate a takedown, demonstrates where the opponent is weak and is thus easily thrown.

6.2.13 – We imagine the diagram at our opponent's feet and orient ourselves with the voids available to us. In this case, we choose the void to our left for expediency and begin to direct our opponent to that void.

6.2.14 – The opponent falls exactly as predicted by the void, shown to us in the diagram we had imagined at his feet.

Questions for Self-Study
Prompts for Further Consideration & Training

1. What are the mechanics which allows you to increase the power of basic kicks without acquiring additional muscle mass?

2. Getting kneed to the outside or inside of the thigh is painful enough, but where else could you connect with this lateral knee strike?

Application 7

Application 12
...e Leg
(...he Other Leg)
Steps 40-42

24

23

Application 7
Rising Fists Boxing System
Steps 22-24

22

Rising Fists Boxing System
Application 7: Bassai Dai Steps 22–24

What inspired Bassai Dai? Why do we practice it the way we do? How is it related to other systems?

It was inevitable after many years of practice that we—the JDK—would seek out connections to other systems. If any were found, we could consider any such system cousin to our own and the JDK would be a branch of a larger family tree.

While Bassai clearly traces back to Okinawa in the 18th century, there are few clues from before that time.

We know that Okinawans "were forbidden by Japan to trade freely overseas" but "quite consciously blended cultural elements and institutions drawn from China and Japan and from Southeast Asia" (Kerr 210). In that era, there's no doubt Okinawan pugilists would find affinity with *Fuzhou's Baihe Quan* (白鶴拳)—aka White Crane Kung Fu—they're practically neighbors. But more importantly, the gravity exerted by the Shaolin Monastery (少林寺) in Henan Province would mean that Okinawans would be familiar with the well-entrenched *Wuxing* Five Animal (五行) styles near Henan and its forms.

Bassai itself presents no verifiable links to Chinese systems. However, from a casual inspection, Bassai exhibits hints of *Wuxing* Leopard's "half fist" and scattered techniques from Tiger and Crane.

Characteristics of Leopard Kung Fu include "speed and angular attack" ("Leopard Kung Fu"). Angular attack perfectly describes our own attempts to find innovative angles of entry to bypass the opponent's defense and coverage.

An analysis of Application 7 also suggests Leopard Kung Fu, which has movements similar to a *Chishou* Sticking Hands (黏手) exercise. Partners training with Sticking Hands connect through intertwined arms to disrupt the other's center of gravity.

The Sticking Hands exercise develops sensitivity through physical connection for close quarter combat which allows us to better predict an opponent's intentions in order to create a tactical advantage.

How do we learn to do this? We register any push or pull from the opponent. Feel the change in his body

7.1.1 – The opponent has crossed the gap, breached our fence, and presents a double shove or grab.

7.1.2 – We slam our forearms together against his as we drop our weight into a stable stance...

7.1.3 – Then immediately bounce our fists right up into his neck or jawline.

7.1.4 – If the opponent continues to hold us, we circle under and out from between his arms to break his grip.

7.1.5 – We draw down on his arms and lock onto his upper arms by folds of skin, muscle or sleeves (skin or muscle is very painful).

7.1.6 – Locked firmly onto our opponent's arms, we use a knee kick to his pelvis or groin to break his balance.

7.1.7 – As our opponent tries to correct his posture, we release our grip…

7.1.8 – And drive either one or both of our forearms with our body weight into his clavicle.

7.1.9 – We then wrap our arm around his neck to control his upper body, and…

7.1.10 – Shifting our body outwards, we step outside of his opposite leg for a leg reap throw

7.1.11 – The opponent has his balance broken. At this point, we could switch our hand position to accelerate his head into the floor.

7.1.12 – Rolling around on the floor now becomes an option only because we dropped him nicely.

as he tenses. Become aware of his rhythm. We learn through practice how to interpret these changes in our opponent to divine his intentions. Once we discern them, we launch our offensive.

The first series of movements in this application (Pics 7.1.4–7.1.12) features twin inside forearm hammer strikes to the opponent's arms. In the setup, the opponent is either performing a double lapel grab or a push. The blade of the forearms cut inwards and downwards, drawing the opponent toward our center of gravity (Pic 7.1.2). As we make the initial connection, we bounce our fists back up, striking the opponent's neck, jaw or face (Pic 7.1.3).

The strike reels the opponent back and we suck him towards us by clawing down his arms to grasp him by the upper arms (Pic 7.1.5). We can grasp him by his clothing, skin or the muscles in his biceps. Clothing is easiest to grab if it is available. The latter points, however, are very painful for our opponent.

If the opponent has a grip on us, we circle under his arms to break the grip, and then claw-grab the inside of his upper arms (Pic 7.1.4) and lock onto his clothing, skin or biceps.

Once we have latched onto our opponent's upper arms, we execute a knee strike into the hip or pubic region to weight him back on his heels. In response, he bends forward at the waist, jutting his head toward us and stretching his arms out for balance (Pics 7.1.6–7.1.7).

We then drive the blades of our forearms sharply against his clavicles. Our strike drives forward with our body weight behind it, smashing his collarbone (Pic 7.1.8).

The American Academy of Orthopaedic Surgeons says that once a clavicle injury occurs, the opponent may experience an "inability to lift the arm" (Githens & Lowe). Most clavicle fractures are sustained through a blow to the shoulder; for example, from a fall or auto accident (Githens & Lowe). We, however, directly target the clavicle to "switch off" the opponent's arm.

The opponent is off-balanced and stunned by our initiative. We shift one side of our body close, grab him around the neck and shoulder (Pic 7.1.9), move his balance to the outside of his base, and then perform a hip throw or take out the support of his farthest leg (Pics 7.1.10–7.1.12). ∎

7.2.1 – The opponent hasn't got the message. We batter his pelvis with knee strikes.

7.2.2 – We attack his clavicles as before, then clinch around the back of his neck and pull his head forward and down.

7.2.3 – We shift to the side of the opponent and drive our forearm into the carotid artery in the side of the opponent's neck.

Alternate Application 1: Sink His Head into His Base

This second group of photos (Pics 7.2.1–7.2.9) shows an alternate ending which may be useful in situations where we need a momentary shield between us and another combatant.

We attack the opponent with both arms in tandem up to the unusual forearm strike to break the clavicle bones (Pics 7.2.1–7.2.2).

We then maneuver to the side of the opponent, transition into a neck control to drop the opponent's head, and fire off a vertical elbow—right into the closest side of his neck (Pic 7.2.3). The neck control is accomplished by the natural use of a double arc hand press throughout this sequence.

7.2.4 – We snap the opponent's head down with both hands and meet it with an upward shin kick to the face.

7.2.5 – Our kicking leg hooks to the back of the opponent's nearest foot as we press down on his neck, hyperflexing it.

7.2.6 – Another angle showing the hook of the opponent's leg and hyperflexing of his neck using a double arc hand press.

7.2.7 – Pushing the opponent's hyperflexed head slowly through to his hips causes the opponent to fall backwards awkwardly. Snapping it faster causes more damage to the neck.

7.2.8 – The opponent flops hard onto the floor. At this point we could stomp on his ankle, knee, or groin to finish him.

7.2.9 – In this example, we choose to spare our opponent and walk away.

The rising knee from the *kata* is re-envisioned as a strike to the opponent's face with the top of our shin to cater for distance. It makes connection while we hold the opponent's head in place (Pic 7.2.4). Like we're dropkicking a football.

We retain contact with the opponent's head and finish the sequence by attacking the closest leg and his support structure. We press his head firmly down—chin to his chest—to hyperflex the neck as we hook his nearest supporting leg (Pics 7.2.5–7.2.6).

To complete the takedown, we continue to press the opponent's head through to his hips, creating a compression and sharp flexion of the neck before we force him to the floor (Pics 7.2.7–7.2.8). ■

Alternate Application 2: Extrapolation of the Spinning *Dantian* Throw

For the second alternate application (Pics 7.3.1–7.3.8), we find ourselves working—or have maneuvered to be—inside the opponent's guard.

In this application, we use the drop and lift of our hands against a jab+cross from our opponent (Pics 7.3.2–7.3.3), a double windshield wiper effect to neutralize these strikes. Rotating our trunk and shoulders to enter the fray lets us choose which arm connects with the opponent's first strike.

(The next few movements [7.3.4–7.3.6] extrapolate from the JDK *dantian* throw, a method to off-balance an opponent. See pages 78-79 for more information.)

We next grip his shoulders, which allows us to manhandle him and quickly pull him forward and downward into a mid-level knee strike (Pic 7.3.5).

The opponent naturally tries to backpedal and pull upward out of our grip, so we pop a double elbow strike upwards right into his chest (Pic 7.3.6). Together, these snap him back up, making him top-heavy.

Suddenly we shift our strategy, level change, target his hip, and disappear into the pocket. We move our head under his radar, and slice a forearm heavily downwards into the fold of his hip (Pic 7.3.7). Depending on the situation, we may reach down with our rear hand or trap the back of his leg with our foot. The opponent's structure collapses and he crumples to the floor in an angle of descent which makes it difficult to breakfall properly. ■

7.3.1 – We square up with the opponent and lift our hands in a cautionary manner. We say we don't want any trouble.

7.3.2 – Unable to read our opponent, we bring both hands down to deflect and shield against his first initiative.

7.3.3 – We immediately use the rising fists technique to deflect his secondary tool—maybe even to drive our fists into his face.

7.3.4 – We reach for his shoulders, contemplate the headbutt, and drag him into a knee strike.

7.3.5 – The strike lands on his pelvis or leg, pushing his hip back and bending him forward.

7.3.6 – Either both or one of our elbows smash him upwards in the chest and pops him upright.

7.3.7 – In a surprise move, we disappear from view, drop to his hip and drive a lower block directly into the corner of his pelvis...

7.3.8 – Which collapses his structure and sends him along with his center of gravity into the void.

Spinning *Dantian* Throw
The Oral Transmission of Body Mechanics

Our summary analysis of Bassai and the potential influence of Chinese systems presents us with an opportunity to both introduce another concept steeped in Chinese tradition and acknowledge the influence of Shaolin thought within the form.

As we played with applications in the standup clinch position, we tested an esoteric soft-style throw which arose from a discussion about the manipulation of energy around our *dantian*. The use of an invisible force to magically repel an opponent would be nothing short of a miracle! But we suspended disbelief as we experimented and ran with the physical elements of the technique.

Dantian is a Chinese concept for the point where *chi*,

our life force, originates in the body. Known as *hara* in Japanese, Western systems simply identify it as one's center of gravity, located approximately three inches below the navel.

A *dantian* throw starts with a neck or shoulder control similar to what is shown in Pics 7.3.4–7.3.5. We latch onto the opponent's neck and pull vertically down toward our feet, weighting the opponent just forward of his base. An Internal stylist would say that we are spinning our *dantian* backwards and allowing *chi* to flow backwards through our arms into the *dantian*.

Once the opponent resists or attempts to counter this downward pull, we redirect the force from downwards to forwards, flinging our hands ahead of us, parallel to the floor. An Internal stylist would say we are now spinning the *dantian* vertically forward, channeling our *chi* directly ahead of us.

The move results in the opponent's head snapping backwards. Like a coiled spring, the potential energy within his body is released from the clinch and he is flung away. He pops back and out of his base in such a dramatic and eccentric fashion it is impossible for him to recover. Soft stylists would simply say we have "floated" him off his base.

Photos we have taken of this phenomenon look like staged hocus pocus. To be honest, we retrofitted a hard-style explanation using a double elbow strike to the chest (Pic 7.3.6) so that hard-stylist fighters would be less likely to question the phenomenon.

However, this is the progression of soft-style training: "The External informs the Internal and the Internal informs the External." The external or physical moves show what is possible. And when a base of understanding has been established, we increase sensitivity and efficiency, and reduce raw strength. Eventually we are able to manhandle an opponent with little need for muscular strength. We simply coordinate good structure, direction, and our kinetic chain, using *chi* as a mnemonic device.

The *dantian* spinning backward and forward isn't a schematic for a human power generator. It's a visual analogy to help coordinate the movement of compound muscle groups. The mnemonic use of *chi* flow and *dantian* is a very clever device for the oral transmission of body mechanics and physical processes. It is an elegant yet covert method of instruction.

In other words, while it is possible to micromanage students with detailed instruction on posture, stance and technique, *dantian* and *chi* flow are the only visuals needed for a well-trained practitioner to learn to disrupt an opponent's balance by using the opponent's natural and predictable responses—his own energy—against him.

For our purposes, the brief introduction we have provided and the clarity of one's own tactical strengths are a good place to start for students to begin to develop a game plan.

We encourage students with an interest in the concepts discussed here to seek masters in the internal arts for guidance and specialty training to better understand, develop or enhance the skills demonstrated in these applications.

Students, however, should not expect this training in the internal arts to be just an afternoon endeavor. ∎

Questions for Self-Study
Prompts for Further Consideration & Training

1. It is often said that Karate is a one hit/one kill system. If we put aside this tactic, what techniques would you use to overwhelm an opponent?

2. When do you think such a strategy—one hit/one kill—would be appropriate?

Application 8

Application 8
Pushing & Pulling
Steps 25a-26

25a

25b

26

pponent

40

Pushing & Pulling
Application 8: Bassai Dai Steps 25b–26

Aikido.

Beautiful. Balletic.

The Aikido techniques I still teach have been held close to my heart for over 30 years, but it took me a long time to assimilate them into the JDK method. Reviewing them every so often makes clear what we do, inasmuch as what we don't do.

Soft style techniques shift the opponent's center of gravity to the outside of his base, or causes the opponent to crumble on his base. For instance, *kokyunage*, *kaitenage*, *tenchinage*, and *iriminage* are techniques taught early in Aikido to off-balance an opponent outside his base.

Once we understand how such techniques work, and when we have the sensitivity to read our opponent's skeletal structure, takedowns become an incredibly useful skill in our toolkit.

They will not look like picture-perfect Aikido, but that's mostly because our opponent is not going to be as compliant or as collaborative as an Aikido training partner. All we need to start are those individual techniques and the training to familiarize ourselves with how the mechanics of them work.

Similar to the concept of *kuzushi*, or the unbalancing we talked about in Application 1, Aikido techniques work because we set the opponent up to fail. A takedown or lock becomes possible when circumstances fit or when we orchestrate it to happen.

Some *kata* analysts believe that turns in a form signify that we've finished the opponent or thrown him and have "reset" ourselves to deal with the next opponent.

A takedown, however, can occur at any point. With any move. So long as we set the opponent up with our *kuzushi*, the takedown will occur when it must. Not at an arbitrary point within *kata*.

In this application for Steps 25b–26 from Bassai, we assume the opponent has crossed hands with us. We could be in gridlock because of a lapel grab or a double hand push or if both wrists are being held (Pics 8.1.2–8.1.3). With our hands occupied, an extended heel thrust unbalances the opponent's hip or hyper flexes his support leg (Pic 8.1.4). This moves his center of gravity back onto his heels, with his body bending forward.

The opponent doesn't want this at all. He attempts to stand or at least to pull back from us. From here, we free the one hand and give him what he wants—we help him stand up—then push his head back and redirect it like a steering wheel in a circular path (Pics 8.1.5–8.1.7). These movements, which mirror the lower block in the pattern, shifts him upright, and then flat spins him out of his base.

Against a live non-compliant opponent, we can do this with either hand. Meaning, if he reads our first motion, freezes up and doesn't go easily in the one direction, we can change tact. Switch hands, use his own resistance against him (as we have done in other applications), and spin him in the opposite direction. Eventually, his balance moves laterally from the back of his heels to the left or right of his body. And without a footprint to tripod his center of gravity, he ends up falling to the floor.

To ensure the ease of this takedown, we jerk his arms forward forcefully as we push his hips back with our heel. This is a gimmick, of course. The throw doesn't

Application 9

29　　28b　　28a　　27b

Attack the Hip to Drop the Opponent
Application 9: Bassai Dai Steps 27a–31

This application focuses on the steps leading up to and including the three consecutive Figure 9 down blocks (Pattern Diagram, Steps 27a–31).

The Figure 9 block is often presented by both Japanese and Korean stylists as a joint attack or an arm break.

But wouldn't an arm break be easier if we used our body as a fulcrum against the elbow to create torque via a sharp hip twist?

For someone of my stature—just 5' 7" and on the lighter side of 150 lbs—that is to say, someone of small stature—larger compound muscles are a much better and effective choice to break the elbow.

We must remember also that the average Japanese man in the late 1890s—a short time after Bassai Dai was created in Okinawa—stood only about 5' tall (Roser). We must also remember that, historically, Okinawans have been shorter on average than their Japanese counterparts ("By Prefecture").

This small average stature of the period which gave us Bassai *kata* further underscores the difficulty of teaching the Figure 9 block as a joint break.

Thus, at the JDK, we don't teach the Figure 9 block as an arm break.

In truth, I practiced the Figure 9 block for years without having a tactical use for it. Sometimes, the value of a single technique eludes us for a host of different reasons. And it's not like I haven't seen what other instructors do. There are several applications taught by others which do have merit. But the solution we use at the JDK has to fit our ability and our needs.

In this application, the Figure 9 movement plays the part of a takedown in a sequence that helps gap-close on the opponent, stop a secondary attack, and drop him off his base.

Once more, "a block is more than a block."

We offer two variations of this application: one for inside the opponent's arms; one for outside.

General Application

The initial hand extension seeks connection—maybe it's a deflection or maybe an adherence to a limb. Or it's to occupy the opponent's visual field. Or deliver a vertical striking technique to the head or neck region. The initial tactic finds the connection, and a crescent kick is fired, stopping the opponent in his tracks. Timed just after we make initial connection, the swinging inward crescent targets anywhere from the hip or trunk to stop his forward movement (Pics 9.1.2–9.1.3).

Although the inward crescent kick might have a flight path that swings somewhat laterally, we are able to direct the power transmission into the opponent at the point of impact with the extension of the leg and hip. The crescent kick here is done closer-in and thus the leg is not necessarily fully extended at the point of impact.

We need not get overly hung up on the flight path of the crescent kick. Fly the weapon into place and jar the opponent. Transfer his center of gravity back into his heels.

As we drop our leg to the ground and step in, we tuck

Inside the Opponent's Arms

9.1.1 – We square up with the opponent.

9.1.2 – We read an initiative coming on the same side and extend our hand to meet it.

9.1.3 – We stay connected with his arm and fire a crescent kick toward his hip, rocking his COG (center of gravity) backwards.

9.1.4 – As he tries a cross, we crash into his chest with a horizontal elbow, wrecking his ability to rotate his shoulders.

9.1.5 – While he is immobilized, we immediately drop a heavy forearm into his pelvis.

9.1.6 – We push our shoulder forward, pull on his arm, and press on his hip to rotate him laterally outside his base.

9.1.7 – The opponent pivots while falling. We can now immobilize him or make our escape.

Outside the Opponent's Arms

9.2.1 – Seems we have been here before.

9.2.2 – The initiative comes from the opposite side. We adjust our bearing to ride its trajectory and keep in contact with it.

9.2.3 – We fire a crescent kick into his hip to rock his COG backwards

9.2.4 – Stepping forward, our elbow collides with his tricep, sending a shockwave into the arm.

9.2.5 – To guard against a cross, we flex his wrist towards us and press our elbow forward to attack his shoulder joint.

9.2.6 – As before, we slip down and slam a forearm into his hip. This rocks his COG onto his heels.

9.2.7 – We hook his lead leg, connect our knee with his, then lunge forward through his hip.

9.2.8 – He falls, totally destabilized, and regrets his latest life decisions.

our chin, maybe even change levels. The last thing we want is our head sticking out like a Whack-A-Mole. With our initial arm extension still adhering to part of the opponent's body, we start to swing our rear hand through with an elbow strike to the body (Pic 9.1.4).

This concept to strike the body, robbing the opponent's ability to generate power, is taken broadly from Chinese martial arts (Wang), *Bajiquan* in particular ("Adam Hsu"). This approach controls the opponent's shoulder line and interferes with his upper limbs and center of gravity and negates counter strikes.

For a split second the opponent has no chance to launch counterstrikes.

Inside the Opponent's Arms

If we are inside the opponent's arms, we slam the elbow strike between the opponent's sternum and ribs. We don't want him caving in our temple with a hook from that rear hand! The strike into that area of the chest stops his shoulder rotation immediately as the shock vibrates into his skeleton, freezing his upper body in place (Pic 9.1.4). This is *sen sen no sen* (先の先)—literally, "to anticipate an attack before the attack"—a preemptive initiative to stop a secondary strike before it even happens ("Sen").

Next, we drop our Figure 9 heavily to the opponent's hip onto his iliac crest (Pic 9.1.5)—see page 48 for a diagram of the iliac crest. This works almost like the move in Application 7, except the Figure 9 application attacks the side of his hip. The force is sent into his base—his body caves, his head juts forward, and the legs start to buckle. If he is able to resist or adapt, we put our shoulder into the extended limb, and then crankshaft his upper body as a single unit into the ground (Pic 9.1.6).

Outside the Opponent's Arms

If we're outside the opponent's arms, we use the elbow strike to cut his tricep then flex his forearm to attack the lead shoulder joint (Pic 9.2.4). With his front shoulder jammed and unable to move freely, his rear hand can't pop us in the face. If we wanted, we could even take it further, using the flexion to create a shearing force in the joint of the lead shoulder (Pic 9.2.5).

We then drop the Figure 9 heavily to the opponent's hip onto his iliac crest (Pic 9.2.6). His balance crumbles as described previously and in Application 7. To counter any resistance or adaption at this point, we shift our center of gravity toward his structure and through it (Pic 9.2.7). This sends him backwards, outside his base, and down into the void (Pic 9.2.8)—see pages 69-70 for an explanation of the void.

Dropped onto the hip, the Figure 9 becomes a pile driver. The opponent expects some strike or counter at face level, but such an attack never comes.

In fact, his visual field empties of incoming strikes and the defender disappears down into the pocket. Suddenly, a strange 150 lbs. of heaviness slams downward on the side of his pelvis. There's no time to adapt to the resulting displacement of his hips. And without something to hold onto, his center of gravity shifts out past his base. He cannot help but fall.

Receiving an opponent's attack and applying the Figure 9 motion in this manner destabilizes even the most fervent of believers. ∎

Questions for Self-Study
Prompts for Further Consideration & Training

1. Why is it appropriate to have both lethal and non-lethal techniques in your toolkit?

2. In this application, we work on the outside of the strike and establish elbow control. What else can be done with that elbow control?

Application 10

Application 10
Mountain Strike Strips His Guard
Steps 32-37b

33

34

Opposite View

37b

37a

Mountain Strike Strips His Guard
Application 10: Bassai Dai Steps 32–37b

The Mountain Strike in Bassai as a double punching attack is one of the more esoteric techniques in the traditional arsenal (Pattern Diagram, Steps 32–37b).

We've never seen any fighter or video of a fighter who uses both hands to simultaneously strike his opponent in the manner of the Mountain Strike.

But it happens in *Wuxia* movies all the time.

Martial artists who insist that the double-punch is effective in real life should pressure test the technique against a counter puncher. We believe he will soon come to share our skepticism about the double-punch.

The Mountain Strike is so called because the hand position looks like a *yama*, or 山, the Japanese *kanji* for mountain. In training, the arms chamber at the hip away from the opponent; there's a swing of the arms over, forward and down so the fists strike at the same time on the same vertical plane, one above the other. Held this way, the double strike resembles the *kanji* turned on its side.

As we understand it, the Mountain Strike is an attack along the vertical axis. Like a wave, it rolls forward and strikes from above the shoulder, and breaks over the opponent like a rush of whitewater. When we reverse that motion, the backwards rolling of the arms strike to the opponent's gut or upwards toward the chin from under the arm.

In this application, the flight path of our lead forearm swings up, over and down to strip the opponent's lead guard or deflect his lead jab downward. Our secondary tool then crests over-the-top to strike the opponent's head or neck.

Trapping or Stripping the Lead Arm

10.1.1 – The opponent has closed the gap to be within striking range.

10.1.2 – We have our fence up and take the initiative—driving our lead hand forward to his centerline. Our knuckles are inverted, palm up, and occupy his visual field.

10.1.3 – As our forearm traps his lead, we turn the tables... and deliver an over-the-shoulder strike without encountering any resistance.

Trapping the Lead Weapon, Deflecting the Secondary

10.2.1 – Our opponent is nothing if not persistent. He squares up again, preparing to attack.

10.2.2 – We trap his lead hand and prepare for the secondary attack.

10.2.3 – We disengage our trapping hand and, moving obliquely, reach to the outside of the incoming tool.

10.2.4 – We deflect his secondary tool, opening his right side to attack.

10.2.5 – Our rear hand fires over his shoulder into the side of his head or face.

If needed, we can step forward, trap his arm with our left forearm, and fire another over-the-shoulder strike with our right hand. Or we can grab his hair and yank his head backward into the void.

The big swing of our lead arm ending with the characteristic palm up position is wasted if this movement is only conceived as a strike.

While the bottom hand can, theoretically, strike in tandem with the top hand, its value as a trap or parry is highly prized at the JDK.

The arc of the lead arm can be liberally used to trap one or both of the opponent's arms or jam his body (Pics 10.1.1-10.1.3). If we've already trapped the opponent's lead guard, the circular over, forward and downward motion can be used to deflect an oncoming secondary tool (Pics 10.2.1-10.2.5).

Power is generated by expanding our body from the rear leg, through the trunk and into our striking arm. This kinetic chain resembles the circumference of a wheel, an analogy that draws a line starting from the back leg, up the side of the body, through the shoulder and into the striking tool. The power strike rockets in over the shoulder, making defense against it difficult

(Pics 10.1.3, 10.2.5 & 10.3.1).

Once we've landed this initial strike, we can launch the bottom hand in an upward cycle to land an upset punch into the opponent, driving into his midsection or upward to his jaw in the form of an uppercut.

If our initial strike strike doesn't land, however, or if the distance to the opponent opens, we step forward and apply the same trapping technique again but on the opposite side of the opponent. We can repeat the up, over, and downward trapping motion as needed, stepping each time, until our strike lands.

When we formally train the Mountain Strike, the hands chamber at the hip away from the opponent. In practice, however, we can reduce the size of the chambering motion to increase our speed. We don't need to start the huge circular motion from the opposite hip. We can truncate the motion instead and start from wherever our hands happen to be positioned, then aim the flight path to gain the most control over the opponent's guard.

There is otherwise minimal variation to the technique. The cycling forward of our hands is repeated until we deliver the payload. ∎

Vertical + Horizontal Axes

Many years ago, it was described to me that the Chinese martial art of *Xing Yi Quan* (形意拳) focuses on owning the opponent's vertical axis, and that its sister art *Bagua Zhang* (八卦掌) focuses on circular attacks around the opponent's horizontal axis. Both of these subspecialties were well-established at the time Bassai was conceived; their tactics would have been known to the architects of Bassai.

Since the JDK practices the Mountain Strike as an attack up and down the vertical axis, we must not

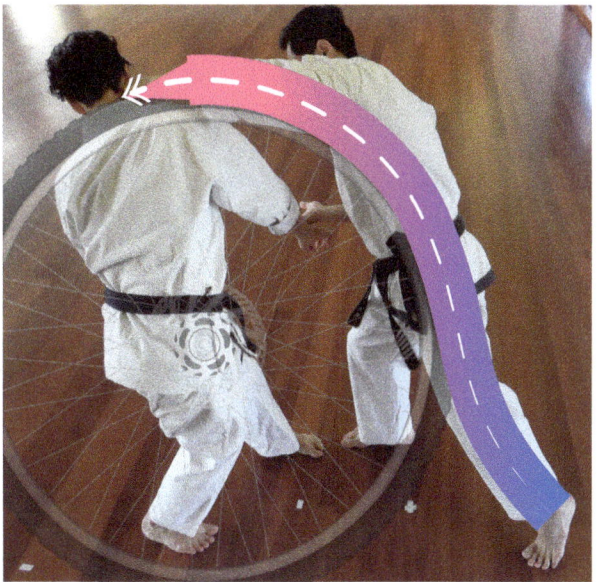

10.3.1 – In this application, the kinetic chain resembles the circumference of a wheel. The chain starts at the back leg, moves up the side of the body, through the shoulder and into the striking tool, delivering the power strike.

forget to be flexible and open-minded as we study this or any technique. Once we have a clear understanding of the vertical nature of the Mountain Strike, we should also consider the usefulness of the horizontal axis, the literal polar opposite.

This requires us once more to make a conceptual leap, just as we had in Application 8 when we described a list of Aikido techniques as the same conceptual takedown but simply in different directions.

This Mountain Strike application prompts us to chunk together what at first may seem to be disparate techniques. The idea is to blend combos that blitz attack the vertical, as we do for the Mountain Strike, then switch over to a horizontal focus and continue our attack.

We can easily chunk together this application of a Mountain Strike with concepts and applications presented earlier in this book, such as the Aikido takedown techniques from Application 8 (see pages 83-85) and the concept of the void (see pages 69–70).

Once we've loosened up the opponent, we can step through, circling to take his back. The downward cycling technique that was previously a trap now drags his head back and down into the void. As he's peeled off-balance, we can then punch downward to accelerate his fall against the ground.

In this example, the techniques are simply both arms flowing in concentric circles—and we then send this along whichever axis targets the opponent's undefended openings.

It seems logical to us to train like this: Search out openings anywhere along the two axes and combine familiar, well-trained techniques to take advantage of them. Attack, control, swarm or bypass the opponent's arm and strike. ∎

Questions for Self-Study
Prompts for Further Consideration & Training

1. If you had to group techniques that complemented each other along the same axis, such as this segment of Bassai, which techniques would you choose?

2. How can we improve our sensitivity to better read the opponent's intention?

Application 11

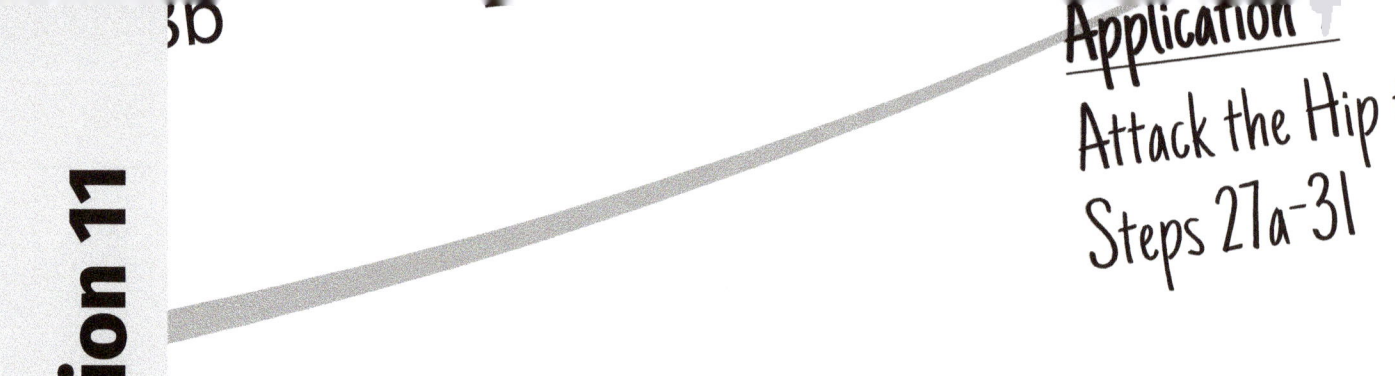

Application
Attack the Hip t
Steps 27a-31

38a   38b   39a   39b

Application 11
Big Scoop Limb Control
Steps 38a-39b

Bassai (拔塞), also Passai, is the name of a group of kata p
  styles of Japanese and Korean martial arts, including

Big Scoop Limb Control
Application 11: Bassai Dai Steps 38a–39b

Why would a hard stylist need to apply locks? Or limb control? Or takedowns and throws? Why would an unarmed fighting system need for anything other than kicks, punches, and elbow strikes?

What should we do when faced with a committed assailant, weapon in hand? Dependent on the weapon, if the attacker isn't downed decisively, his next move might find us bleeding out from multiple cuts and stab wounds. Or with our skull busted open on the concrete.

Neither are great outcomes for us.

Students need skills which include de-escalation techniques and immobilization of the aggressor. They need the wherewithal to assess each situation as it unfolds. They don't need more of the hard-style one-hit-one-kill rhetoric. In the heat of combat, percussive strikes such as kicks and punches do not consistently put down a committed attacker. Plus, not all bad things are done by bad people. Therefore we need a range of skills appropriate for each situation and the level of force required.

One of JDK's philosophies when teaching weapon defense skills to those young-in-the-arts focuses on controlling and immobilizing the weapon arm. This approach is easy to learn, slows down the encounter, greatly reduces the chance that the weapon will be used to injure us, and is a way to inch the encounter toward a more predictable and preferable outcome. The JDK approach is also easier to remember—and apply—than a flurry of movements often demonstrated by knife defense experts.

This application uses the big scooping blocks near the end of Bassai (Pattern Diagram, Steps 38a–39b) for both empty-hand and weapons defense—knife defense in this case—to achieve gap closing and connection, limb control, limb destruction, and finally the manipulation of the opponent's center of gravity—whether from inside or outside his reach.

Our initiative begins by surging toward one side of the opponent—either inside or outside to gain the advantage of two unobstructed arms. At the same time, we capture his lead guard or weapon arm (Pics 11.1.1 & 11.2.1).

We call this sudden surge and strategic placement of our arms *swarming* because, like a large group of attacking insects such as bees or locusts, it confuses the victim because the attacking tool(s) or direction(s) cannot be readily discerned.

We follow this gap closing and limb control with an elbow-to-elbow strike, a particularly nasty surprise (Pics 11.1.1 & 11.2.2). The elbow strike may injure the joint and cause muscle spasms

Altogether, this swarming in, the separation of his arm from his body, the pain and shock, draws the assailant's focus and disrupts his intent to harm us.

While we don't actually tear off the opponent's arm, we describe the sensation for him as "separation" because, as we capture the arm, we seek to move it away from his body and reduce his control over it. The better we capture and control his arm, the less control he has over it and the greater its degree of separation.

Our elbow strike impacts the sensitive upper arm, bicep or elbow and appropriately tensions his limb (Pics 11.1.2 & 11.2.3). This pulls his center of gravity off-kilter. The result—the opponent goes to his toes and the pain in his arm wrecks his fight sense.

We continue to close the gap by moving closer to the opponent. If required, we can improve our grip on the controlled limb and/or liberally strike to the opponent's neck to further loosen him up.

In truth, we can grip the offending arm anywhere from the wrist to the bicep, so long as we better manage our

Inside the Arm

11.1.1 – We surge to the inside of the opponent, grab the offending arm, and attack the inside of his elbow or bicep with a sharp elbow strike, moving our head offline.

11.1.2 – We extend our elbow strike onto his shoulder or atop of his bicep and apply a light hooking grab to his forearm near the wrist.

11.1.3 – We slice the blade of our forearm into his bicep or shoulder, dropping it toward the ground outside his base.

We have a couple of choices at this point. In this example we drop him in a flat spin forward & outside his stance. We could have just as easily dropped him into the void at his back, farther afield, depending upon circumstances.

11.1.4 – When the integrity of his balance slips, we pull up on his arm to turn him in the air.

11.1.5 – The opponent lands where he belongs—between us and a hard place.

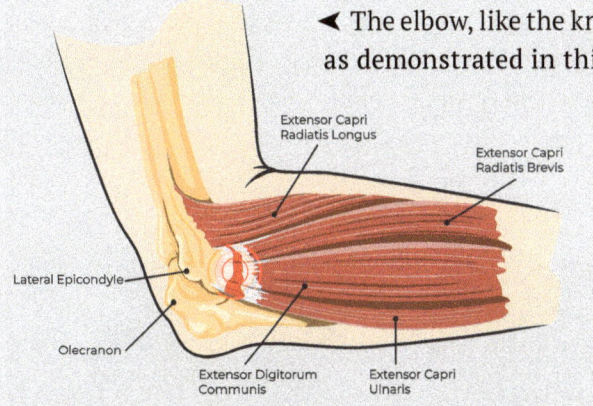

◀ The elbow, like the knee, is susceptible to injury through hyperextension, such as demonstrated in this application and others in this book. Hyperextension doesn't always cause immediate pain. In some minor hyperextension injuries, pain may develop later ("Hyperextended Elbow"). If severe injury or dislocation is suspected, seek immediate medical attention. Microtrauma, which is cumulative in nature, may occur from repeated minor hyperextensions, as well as locking the arm or leg straight during punching and kicking during *kata* practice. "While the snapping sound of the Ghi (sic) is rather satisfying in nature, the rotation of the wrist at the end of a strike is causing microtrauma to the elbow, and this trauma tends to be cumulative in nature" (Klein). It can't be said often enough. **Train with care!**

control over the arm so the opponent cannot yank it free or piston it to regain control.

If the opponent wields a knife, it's best to swarm the offending arm, wrap it up with our entire arm for maximum control, and seek a higher grip—somewhere just above his elbow. With this higher grip, our arm, elbow and torso help keep the weapon away from our body.

While the application is generally the same whether we choose the inside or outside of the opponent's attacking arm, there are minor differences.

Inside the Arm

Inside his weapon arm (Pics 11.1.1–11.1.5), we saw the blade of our forearm heavily into his deltoid or upper arm. This movement slices our mass tangentially into the structure of his upper body.

Next, we pick a direction away from his center of gravity and off his base—either to the side or to his back where we want him to fall—and point our feet in this direction as well.

The shearing force on his deltoid or upper arm rotates his shoulder, and drops the shoulder line of the grabbed arm (Pic 11.1.3). As his balance starts to move in this direction, we then redirect and start him on a flat spit outside his base (Pic 11.1.4).

We read his reactions at all times. If the initial rotation of his shoulder blade doesn't elicit any opposing motion, we can simply drive in that direction and take him down there. But if there's a shift in his structure and an attempt to recover, then the redirection into a flat spin will challenge his ability to regain his balance.

As the flat spin takes him closer to the ground, we pull up on the arm and slingshot him into the void that's opened up on the ground—right where we dictated (Pic 11.1.5).

Outside the Arm

If we gap close and are outside the opponent's weapon arm (Pics 11.2.1–11.2.6), we strike at his tricep or elbow. If the arm is extended and relaxed, this is a joint attack that might defuse an enthusiastic brawler.

If our strike instead meets a bent arm, the resulting flexion is likely not enough to stop the encounter. In this example, we show the opponent fully absorbing the elbow strike, which we might consider a failure of the application, since the opponent is not neutralized (Pic 11.2.3).

Outside the Arm

11.2.1 – We step to the outside of our opponent and deflect the weapon arm. In our next move, we turn & move off our centerline.

11.2.2 – We grasp the offending arm and attack with an elbow, as before, torquing our body to drive the strike through the joint.

11.2.3 – We drop our elbow down and forward to wedge up the arm. (This example shows pressure against the joint, but this is not essential for the application.)

11.2.4 – We crankshaft his held arm to turn him as we roll and straighten our attacking arm to encourage the roll of his shoulder and drive toward his head.

11.2.5 – We reel him in with a downward circular motion by dropping our weight on his upper arm/shoulder while pulling up on his wrist as high as possible.

11.2.6 – We shift our body weight like a piledriver over his arm — straight out of Aiki 101. The opponent cannot stand in this position unless his structure changes.

But our training has anticipated this failure and we proceed with the lesson taught by our training.

We follow the strike in and crankshaft, or twist, his extended arm. We do this by holding his forearm, and rolling the blade of our forearm upward against the underside of his elbow to bend, or tent, the arm. Though the opponent's hand may initially turn palm side up as in our example, we pronate the opponent's wrist, or wrench it palm down, to twist the arm (Pic 11.2.3–11.2.4). This move resembles wringing a wet towel between our hands.

If successful and the opponent doesn't recover by dropping levels to control the height of his elbow, he will bend over at the waist with his arm extended out from the side of his body, elbow up and thumb down, and he will teeter on his toes (Pic 11.2.4).

Next, we preserve our posture, slide our forearm to his upper arm and, at the same time, position our body structure vertically over his shoulder (Pic 11.2.5). In this position, we press his shoulder as far down to the ground as possible while pulling the offending forearm as high as possible, turning his body (Pic 11.2.6).

At this point, we have successfully limited the opponent's mobility and are now faced once more with choices.

Train the following techniques with care, as the knee joint is easily injured (see page 67).

First, we can continue to seek feedback from and follow the form, i.e. apply the principle of *Shu* (see page 16). Maintaining our posture and pressure on the opponent, we can shift our stance and place the back of a bent leg obliquely in front of his straightened knee joint. We assume in this case that his leg is rooted. If we then straighten our leg and release his arm, this hyperextension of his knee is likely to fell him backwards in an eccentric and dramatic fashion.

To be really nasty, we can position our bent leg in such a way that we ensure that his knee joint breaks. In which case he will collapse in a heap at our feet.

If, however, his knee is not firmly rooted, the pressure on his knee will slip his foot to the rear and he will fall face first to the ground.

This application of stance is Funakoshi's 17th Precept or Lesson for Karate: *kamae wa shoshinsha ni ato wa shizentai* (構は初心者に後は自然体), which means, "Like other forms, you need to apply the stances you've learned as beginners" ("Nijū kun").

This basic forward stance, applied tactically and innovatively, deals with our opponent more elegantly than any punch or kick. Or even trying harder in an attempt to overpower our opponent—which we might not achieve depending on the size of the opponent.

Our second choice, once we have limited our opponent's mobility, is to go off-script from the form as our situation and conscience dictates. We may simply walk him forward and descend him into the ground. Or we could bump him and shift his balance onto the farthest leg, then blow out his knee with a sidekick. If we need to move him as a shield, we can apply a *tenkan*, or turning move, from Aiki 101. This allows both of us to move in a circular orbit, using him as a shield liberally around the room. ∎

Regarding Knife Defense

Knife defense often casts a shadow on traditional martial arts. There's much criticism when knife work is done using unarmed training fundamentals.

I can visualize a particular drill: the instructor, after pairing students, has one student strike vertically downwards with a fist toward the second student's head, and at the right time the second student steps forward and blocks upward against the attacking arm.

If the first student now holds a training knife and stabs at the second student in like manner, the second student uses the exact same movement to block the hand with the knife. They are not taught to make a distinction between the two similar but patently different attacks.

Unfortunately, this scenario does not mesh with reality. In the *dojo*, the assailant moves much slower than an assailant hell bent on doing us harm. The assailant also halts his attacking arm just before the point of impact in order for the victim to train his

Clarification for Knife Defense

11.3.1 – The opponent makes a move and we surge in to make contact before the weapon accelerates to the point of impact.

11.3.2 – We wrap the knife hand and seek a high grip on his arm while moving in. He has turned so we choose to elbow his neck rather than the weapon arm.

11.3.3 – Our priority is to immobilize the knife arm to minimize the threat and gain control over the shoulder. We drop our head to protect against additional strikes.

11.3.4 – We disrupt his center of gravity exactly as before—rolling his shoulder outside his structure, dropping his shoulder line, and then rotating him in the air.

technique. This scenario, of course, is just another way to practice fundamental blocks and strikes.

In real life, our armed attacker will attack far quicker and more voraciously than we like or for which we have prepared. He will strike until he has subdued us and we lay bloody at his feet.

The chaos of a real attack means that the weapon arm isn't going to neatly correspond to any picture perfect technique in any book. Just compare Pic 11.1.2 to Pic 11.3.2.

Rather than look at fundamental blocking techniques, the first lesson most reality-based self-defense instructors share is the reality of knife defense: *We're going to get cut.*

Styles of training which practice a specific skillset within their art develop expertise which cannot be ignored. Just think of Judo as a specialized throwing system, or Escrima as a specialized weapons art.

In other words, far from saying I know better than reality-based instructors, I will gladly take inspiration from combative practices, for they have the urgency to develop practical and effective skills and an obsession for pressure testing their expertise. Their insight pertaining to knife defense is worthwhile.

If you face an attacker holding a knife like an ice pick, you might first notice he's not wearing a *gi*. Next, you might realize he could surge in but could then stop short and sewing-machine-stab your arms and chest.

At which point, my wish is for you to be anywhere else but there, facing the knife.

Or, if you have no other choice, then my wish for you is to swarm the attacker, control his knife arm, and take him down fast and hard!

In the end, knowing technically correct form will not mean we can achieve natural transitions, such as gap closing and connection, as we work this or any application. In a defense situation, we need to allow ourselves to forego picure-perfect and technically correct form. Instead, we need to flow with the movement as we "dance" with the opponent and continue tension or pressure while manipulating him to achieve our desired end.

As we maintain balance and apply bodyweight appropriately, and with effective distancing, structure and leverage—in short, with practice!—these techniques will appear effortless. ∎

Questions for Self-Study
Prompts for Further Consideration & Training

1. Why would we need to attack an opponent's limb?

2. Why would we control the opponent's limb?

Application 12

Application 12
Sweep the Leg
(Then the Other Leg)
Steps 40-42

40

41

practiced in
g Karate,
re several variations
 kata. Both are
 Bassai Sho was
plement Bassai Dai.

42

Rising Fists B

Sweep the Leg (Then the Other Leg)
Application 12: Bassai Dai Steps 40–42

We know that an encounter could end up on the ground. On the same note, if we're into sweeping statements, then most encounters could end up in a standing clinch!

It is in the nature of the opponent to want to hold and control us in place if his initial attack fails. He grabs onto us so he can better hit us. Or stick us if he's armed with a knife. And then there's the possibility we might end up rolling on the sidewalk if our opponent gains the upper hand.

In this example, the opponent gets in our face and creates more forward pressure, so we reach around his neck and snap him forward towards our shoulder. This pulls his upper body forward and down, off-balancing him (Pics 12.1.1–12.1.3).

As the shock of our initiative hits him, there might be a momentary lock-down of muscles throughout his body, freezing him in place and preparing him to respond to the attack. When he next reacts by pulling away, by standing straighter or by shuffling his feet for balance, we drive forward, tipping his head backward, and go for a Judo 101 leg reap takedown (Pics 12.1.4–12.1.6).

But our leg reap fails!

Train for Failure

Nobody wants to fail attempting a technique. It's not that we don't want to take out that first leg. We do.

But preparing for a possible technical failure allows us to predict what is likely to happen in the following moves if we fail in our first attempt. Simply believing a technique is above failure guarantees its failure. Not every time. But at some point. And that's not a good spot for anyone to be where defense is concerned.

This is true about any other application from any pattern or any of our training—if we do not prepare for failure.

If we are committed to *breaking through*, as this book's title suggests, one important lesson to be learned is to train a backup plan for when our initial technique fails.

Because it will. Eventually.

This is an important part of the JDK Methodology—to assume resistance and possible failure, and always train using an if-then-else approach. Such as we find within a flowchart.

In a *complete* lesson, we train for the possibility that our backup move fails, too. If any technique fails,

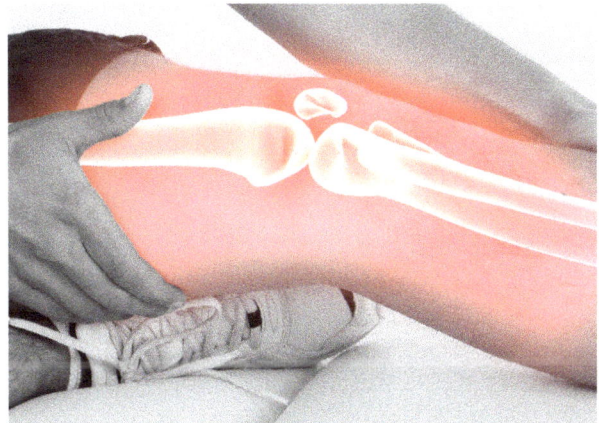

▲ **Remember that the knee—like the elbow or any other joint—can be easily and seriously injured.** Even from forcefully kicking and punching the air in forms (see pages 67 & 103).

be it our first, second, third or etc., then we proceed with another well-practiced backup move to achieve our goal.

Why might our leg reap fail?

It could be that we didn't adequately control our opponent's upper body. A worthy opponent with good reflexes might read our inability to control his upper body, shift his body weight to correct his balance, and lift the leg we intended to sweep (Pic 12.2.1).

12.1.1 – Our opponent seems intent to engage in a standing clinch.

12.1.2 – We reach forward around the opponent's neck and use our left arm to seek a sleeve or skinfold for arm control.

12.1.3 – We drop our weight on the back of his neck to snap him forward. We want him to resist so we make this big and bold.

12.1.4 – As he resists and pulls back, we surge forward and further encourage his resistance by slamming our shoulder into his face and starting a slight rotation by pulling on the captured arm.

12.1.5 – Now we go hip to hip and begin a standard leg reap. Our scenario assumes that our opponent reads this, or that we fail to weight him or tip his head back properly.

12.1.6 – As a result, he pulls his leg before we can execute the leg reap, causing it to fail. We begin our if-then-else protocol.

So, to proceed, we push and pull with our hands, switch our stance to circle around the other side and weight our opponent on the spot using our arms. While he teeters, we launch into our second leg reap on the leg that now supports all his weight (Pics 12.2.2–12.2.3.

Or, as in this example, we off-balance him using a *kokyunage* from Aikido 101—taking his head laterally off his base—dip his shoulder toward the ground, then turn his body so he falls (Pics 12.2.4–12.2.6). ∎

12.2.1 – Our opponent regains his footing after our leg reap failure. But we are prepared. We will do it again on the other side.

12.2.2 – We switch hands and body position on the opponent by lifting his arm then weighting his neck with our left while switching our right to the sleeve or a fold of skin on the opposite arm.

12.2.3 – We attempt the leg reap again on his opposite side. This time it's harder for the opponent to shift out because his new position of stability now points in the wrong direction.

12.2.4 – We hook his leg but don't sweep it. Instead, we lift his arm to flow over his head *à la* Aiki 101.

12.2.5 – Our throw wraps the opponent around our body.

12.2.6 – In this case, fate determines that our opponent lands on the floor.

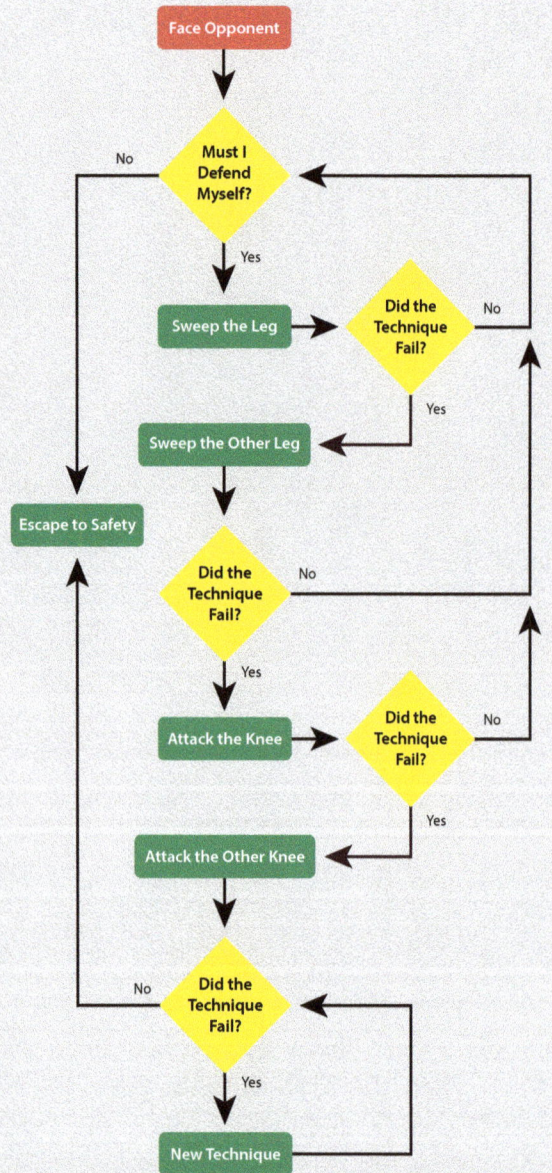

Flowchart for Application 12: Sweep the Leg (Then the Other Leg)

▲ Notice how the if-then-else approach for this application can be described in a flowchart. This chart in particular illustrates two failures to sweep the legs and two failed attacks to the knees—failures for which we have trained. After the last attack to the knee, the process loops as we continue to blitz our opponent in various ways until we finally succeed in taking him down.

The JDK If-Then-Else Protocol

The examples for this application thus far assume that our first leg reap fails but our second takedown succeeds.

What if our second leg reap/takedown fails?

A flowchart is a diagram which directs users step-by-step through a sometimes complicated procedure or process to a desired outcome. Recognized worldwide, flowcharts help document, study, plan, improve and communicate in clear, easy-to-understand terms across diverse disciplines ("What is a Flowchart").

A flowchart specifically directs users to perform tasks in sequence and surveys the success of each task in order to direct users to the next appropriate step based on the status at each step in the procedure.

A loop occurs when a procedure fails and the flowchart directs users to make an adjustment then attempt the procedure again.

Users continue to follow the flowchart until they reach the end of the chart, i.e. the desired outcome.

In our case, the desired outcome of this application is to drop our opponent to the floor by leg sweep or any other familiar method. ∎

If Two Techniques Fail...

Thus far, our opponent has evaded our first leg sweep (Pics 12.3.1–12.3.3).

Now he pulls the second leg away just in time (Pics 12.3.4–12.3.6). So our second reap fails like the first.

As a result, we follow protocol and cycle through with a third technique (Pics 12.3.7–12.3.10). We're now

Application 12: Sweep the Leg (Then the Other Leg)   113

going to blitz the opponent until the job gets done.

Since the opponent has escaped our first two attempts to sweep his leg, he is likely to anticipate another leg reap, so we change it up on him and swing our back leg around to connect with the inside of his opposite knee and hook his leg in place with our foot (Pic 12.3.7). We then flex our knee forward to attack his knee joint and, therefore, his stability.

This tactic needs us to read both where his knee is weak and when his stance is no longer stable.

As always, be cautious when training attacks against the knee (see page 67).

12.3.1 – Let's revisit how JDK trains this particular application using our if-then-else protocol.

12.3.2 – We grasp his neck and sleeve, pull his head forward, pop it back, then go hip to hip for the first leg reap.

12.3.3 – Our opponent pulls his leg out from our leg reap.

12.3.4 – So we circle to the other side and cycle our hands.

12.3.5 – Now we go for the back-up leg reap.

12.3.6 – The opponent pulls his leg for a second time and regains his balance.

Force can be applied judiciously as we play with this concept during training. We can leverage it as deliberately as needed or with more urgency as the opponent's demeanor dictates while our arms continue to push and pull against him to support this takedown (Pics 12.3.8–12.3.10).

What happens if this third attempt fails?

We continue the if-then-else protocol. ∎

12.3.7 – We turn, using our rear leg to attack the inside of the opponent's knee while hooking our foot behind his ankle.

12.3.8 – The force on his leg flexes into his knee, and we steering wheel him like a big truck toward the floor.

12.3.9 – **Train with care!** These techniques attack the knee (see page 67) and this in particular is an unpleasant throw.

12.3.10 – Once he falls, we are free to stomp his ankle, knee, or groin, if needed.

If Our Third Technique Fails…

If the opponent dodges this inside-knee attack, we can apply it again, this time against his other leg, which is now closest to us (Pics 12.4.1–12.4.5).

We turn and swing our rear leg forward as before and connect hard to the inside of the opponent's other knee, then hook our foot behind his ankle and flex our stance to apply pressure to his knee and destabilize him. Pushing and pulling him, with his leg locked in place by our hook, we force him to the ground (Pic 12.4.5). ∎

12.4.1 – We attempt our third knee attack in an effort to fell our opponent.

12.4.2 – The opponent, however, pulls his leg away from the attack.

12.4.3 – We again swing the back leg into his other knee and hook our foot behind his ankle…

12.4.4 – And apply the same attack and takedown to the other side of the opponent!

12.4.5 – Notice how the opponent's leg remains locked by our foot hook.

Remember: Be cautious when training this leg attack or any attack against the knee to avoid injuries (see page 67).

If He Stutter-Steps Instead: Return of the Figure 9 Pile Driver

For our next example, the opponent—rather than fully stepping back (Pic 12.4.2)—stutter-steps instead to avoid our third attack, causing this technique to fail as well (Pics 12.5.1–12.5.2).

Remember that stutter-steps, commonly used in sports, are short, sudden stops and starts to deceive

12.5.1 – Since our two leg reaps failed, we go for the third attack: the inside-knee takedown. But...

12.5.2 – Our opponent pulls his front leg and stutter-steps (instead of stepping back), keeping his front leg forward. Fortunately, we have trained for this failure.

12.5.3 – We swing our back leg forward as before, connecting with the outside of his lead leg. We press our weight into his structure via his knee.

12.5.4 – We level drop to his legs, wrapping our back hand behind his front leg and moving our lead hand to press against the inside of his rear knee.

12.5.5 – We lift his front leg and lunge to push harder against his rear knee until it bends, taking his balance.

12.5.6 – He falls soundly at our feet. It's not a good place for him. But it's been fun for us.

or evade an opponent ("Definition of 'stutter-step'").

In this case, our opponent stutter-steps back but keeps the same foot forward (Pic 12.5.2). Though we expected him to step back, we trained for this failure, too, and continue our if-then-else blitz.

For this example, we drop our head farther into the opponent's lower gate and away from any downward strikes from him.

Now we reach for both of his supports. The closer hand hooks under his closest leg, and the other reaches to push against the inside of his other knee (Pic 12.5.4).

This motion is reminiscent of the Figure 9 application discussed previously as a pile driver on his hips (see Application 9, pages 90–92).

Finally, we lift his closest leg off the floor and lunge forward while pushing against his knee so it bends (Pic 12.5.5). This destabilizes the opponent's base by shifting his structure—irrespective of weight difference—and he falls hard to the ground (Pic 12.5.6). ∎

Did We Mention Safety?

Always maintain training safety. *Judokas* swing their leg to safely lift the opponent's leg and reap the opponent to the floor. However, in our inside-knee attack, we root our leg behind our opponent's foot (Pics 12.4.3–12.4.5). This is very dangerous for our training partner. If we don't cleanly sweep the leg, we could wrench his knee as his body moves but his lower leg remains in place.

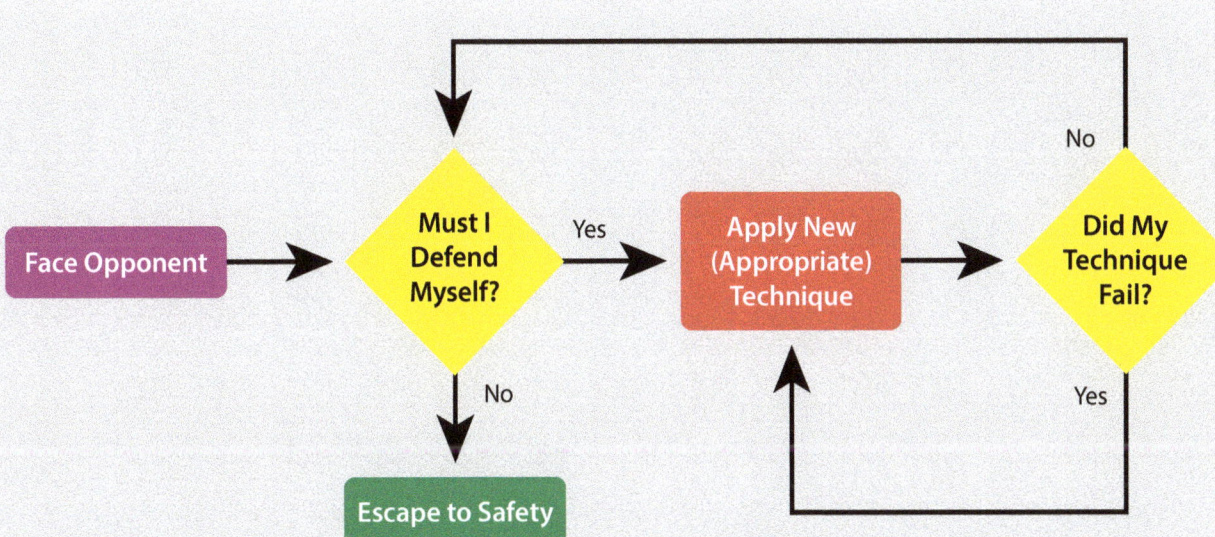

▲ Every lesson in our toolbox—new, old or yet undiscovered—can be trained according to this simplified flowchart. Applications can be plugged into the loop at will until we achieve the desired outcome: the opponent incapacitated such that he is no longer a threat.

This could result in dislocation of his joint and require medical attention.

How likely is this?

We know of an instructor who, practicing one of his forms after class, rooted his support leg during an inward crescent kick and dislocated his knee with a loud, audible *Pop!* Emergency technicians administered a potent painkiller and transported him by ambulance to the nearest hospital. It was nearly a year before he regained full mobility in his knee.

So we have to say that the potential for injury is always present. Even when simply kicking and punching as we perform our *katas* (see page 103). ■

A *Complete* Lesson

At the JDK, we consider a lesson which trains a series of failures—such as this lesson—a *complete* lesson.

We drill this sequence so we are able to blitz attack the opponent's legs, progressing into the various counters if any part of the sequence fails. We simply follow the if-then-else protocol—like a loop in a flowchart—until we realize the desired outcome.

So easy is this approach that we can plug and play any sequence to bookend any other application during a close quarter engagement. The freedom to mix and match combinations like this allows us to plug them into an if-then-else loop very quickly.

That is the true lesson in this chapter. ■

Questions for Self-Study
Prompts for Further Consideration & Training

1. When you are attempting to do a leg takedown as we've described above, how would you gap close and avoid strikes to your head?

2. How might we distract the opponent while attempting a takedown?

Works Cited

"Adam Hsu Baji Chuang Usage Part II." *YouTube*, uploaded by Lancelot Bausley, 11 April 2014, https://www.youtube.com/watch?v=2Vl8DH2_iOw.

"Animal Styles in Chinese Martial Arts." *Wikipedia*, Wikimedia Foundation, 5 November 2022, https://en.wikipedia.org/wiki/Animal_styles_in_Chinese_martial_arts.

"By Prefecture, List of National Average Height of Japanese." *Suku-Noppo*, https://www.suku-noppo.jp/data/average_height_region.html. Accessed 27 Nov 2022.

Clayton, Bruce D. *Shotokan's Secret: The Hidden Truth Behind Karate's Fighting Origins.* Expanded Edition, Black Belt Communications, 2010.

"Definition of 'stutter-step.'" *Collins Dictionary*, https://www.collinsdictionary.com/us/dictionary/english/stutter-step#:~:text=stutter%2Dstep%20in%20American%20English&text=1. Accessed 23 Jan 2023.

Erikkson, Dr. Stefan. "The Knee." *Fight Times*, 17 October 2006, https://magazine.fighttimes.com/the-knee.

"Flow (psychology)." *Wikipedia*, Wikimedia Foundation, 15 Dec 2022, https://en.wikipedia.org/wiki/Flow_(psychology).

Githens, Michael F., and Jason A. Lowe. "Clavicle Fracture (Broken Collarbone)." *American Academy of Orthopedic Surgins*, orthoinfo.aaos.org/en/diseases--conditions/clavicle-fracture-broken-collarbone. Accessed 15 Dec. 2022.

"JKA Techniques: The Inseparable Trinity Lead to Kime." Japan Karate Association., https://www.jka.or.jp/en/about-jka/techniques. Accessed 15 Dec 2022.

Kerr, G. H. *Okinawa: The History of an Island People.* Tuttle Publishing, 2000.

Kim, Bok Man. *Taekwon-do: Origins of the Art: Bok Man Kim's Historic Photospective (1955 - 2015).* Moosul Publishing, 2015.

Klein, David S. "Lateral Epicondylitis-elbow pain (Tennis Elbow-Lateral Epicondylitis)." *Martial Arts Injuries*, 07 December 2008, https://paindoctor.typepad.com/martial_arts_injuries/2008/12/lateral-epicondylitiselbow-pain.html.

"Leopard Kung Fu." *Wikipedia*, Wikimedia Foundation, 19 Nov 2019, https://en.wikipedia.org/wiki/Leopard_Kung_Fu.

Lupika, Sam. "Can What You Eat Affect Your Height?" Livestrong,

"Matsumura Sōkon." *Wikipedia*, Wikimedia Foundation, 3 Oct 2019, https://en.wikipedia.org/wiki/Matsumura_S%C5%8Dkon.

McCarthy, Patrick. *Bubishi: The Classic Manual of Combat.* Tuttle Publishing, 1995.

"Neck Injuries Overview." *Fighting Arts Health Lab*, https://www.fightingartshealthlab.com/combat-arts-injury-recovery/physical-injuries/neck-injuries. Accessed 23 Nov 2022.

"Nijū kun." *Wikipedia*, Wikimedia Foundation, 7 Nov 2019, https://en.wikipedia.org/wiki/Nij%C5%AB_kun.

"Passai." *Wikipedia*, Wikimedia Foundation, 13 Dec 2019, https://en.wikipedia.org/wiki/Passai.

Roser, Max, et al. "Human Height." *Our World in Data*, 2013, https://ourworldindata.org/human-height.

"Sen (先) - Initiative." *Dublin Tomiki Aikido*, https://www.tomikiaikido.ie/go-no-sen-sen-no-sen. Accessed 15 Dec 2022.

"Shuhari." *Wikipedia*, Wikimedia Foundation, 9 May 2019, https://en.wikipedia.org/wiki/Shuhari.

Silverman, Steve. "8 Characteristics that Make a Great Boxer." *The Bleacher Report*, 27 September 2012, https://bleacherreport.com/articles/1349115-8-characteristics-that-make-a-great-boxer.

"Spinal Lock." *Wikipedia*, Wikimedia Foundation, 26 Mar 2020, https://en.wikipedia.org/wiki/Spinal_lock.

"Taekwondo Sine Wave." *Taekwondo Fandom*, https://taekwondo.fandom.com/wiki/Taekwondo_Sine_Wave. Accessed 23 Dec 2019.

"The Different Stages of Knowledge Management." *ISWSA*, http://www.iswsa.org/the-different-stages-of-knowledge-management. Accessed 1 October 2018.

Vullinghs, Jackie. "What is your unfair advantage?" Medium.com, https://medium.com/airtree-venture/what-is-your-unfair-advantage-d547d8055af. Accessed 26 June 2019.

Wang, Lijun. "手法.腿法.擒拿.摔法反制 Self Defense." *YouTube*, uploaded by Wang's Gong Fu, 8 Sep 2018, https://www.youtube.com/watch?v=Yvel25cKJXA.

"What is (sic) a Flowchart?" *Lucidchart*, https://www.lucidchart.com/pages/what-is-a-flowchart-tutorial. Accessed 22 January 2023.

"What to Know About a Hyperextended Elbow." *WebMD*, https://www.webmd.com/fitness-exercise/what-to-know-about-a-hyperextended-elbow. Accessed 18 January 2023.

Worley, John. "Fifty Years of Martial Arts - What I've Seen." *National Karate - Academy of Martial Arts*, 15 April 2019, https://www.nationalkarate.com/fifty-years-of-martial-arts-what-ive-seen.

Yates, Keith D. *The Complete Guide to American Karate and Tae Kwon Do*. Blue Snake Books, 2008.

Yates, Keith D. "A Brief History." *American Karate and Tae Kwon Do Organization*, 2021, http://a-kato.org/styled/index.html. Accessed 5 Nov 2022.

An Interview with Sabumnim Colin Wee

By Mike Swope

Who Is Colin Wee? What is IAOMAS?

"Man's mind, once stretched by a new idea, never regains its original dimensions."
~ Oliver Wendell Holmes

"We are all about instructors doing the best for their students. We want to promote your ideals. We want to reward great behaviour. And we want people to know the benefits of honest and real martial arts training." ~ IAOMAS Web Site

I have known Mr. Colin Wee for several years. We met on Facebook, as I have many other like-minded martial artists. We have exchanged messages, funny stories, personal experiences, personal pain, and ideas about the martial arts. He has published articles in this very magazine. We share many friends on Facebook. Colin, however, is a strange duck. He walks, kicks and strikes like a duck, but he quacks askew. Just a little different. His point of view just a little to the left of what average folks may consider center. His view is sometimes pointed, however, like a scalpel.

I believe that Colin's exceptional views eventually lead to his selection in 2016 as Instructor of the Year for American Karate and Tae Kwon Do Organization (AKATO) based in Dallas, Texas. Nevermind that he has not been an active member of

Colin Wee enjoys teaching and training in all types of locations, including his home garage, gymnasiums, commercial martial arts schools, and the great outdoors – wherever his path leads.

that organization – in the sense that he cannot physically attend their classes or events – for more than two decades. He currently resides in Australia, thousands of miles from the U.S. Nonetheless, he has remained in contact with the organization's leading instructors, including legendary Grandmaster Keith Yates, and often visits AKATO members when he is in the States.

Colin teaches out of his 2-car garage in Perth. He has turned it – with his wife's permission, of course! – into a dojang, with mats on the floors, a variety of bags, and a handful of dedicated students. He teaches a traditional style of Taekwondo. He calls his facility the Joong Do Kwan, or JDK for short. This means "school of the middle way." He also leads the International Alliance of Martial Arts Schools, or IAOMAS, an organization dedicated to the benefit of all who join. Of course, all organizations say they benefit their members. IAOMAS, however, is free to join, collects no dues and sells no products (other than its benefits, of course, which are free).

Colin's father, Bill Wee, was an exceptional and accomplished man himself. I learned that Colin's father is the Father of Archery in Singapore as I prepared the final handful of questions for Colin. Which of course brought on a few more questions. Bill Wee was the top male archer in Singapore for many, many years. He was active in international archery since 1959, founding the Sydney University Archery Club (1959), received the Sydney and New South Wales medals for winning performances, founded the Archery Club of Singapore (1964), represented Singapore and placed in the top 10 of the Games of the Newly Emerging Forces of Cambodia (1966), formed the Archery Association of Singapore) (1967) and acted as its president for most of the period through 2002, served as the Honorary Treasurer of the Asian Archery Federation for many years, and was a respected senior coach and mentor to Sri Lanka, India, Myanmar, China, Bhutan and North Korea. He also founded Bill Wee Agencies, an archery equipment supplier, in Singapore in 1965 and operated the business until his untimely passing in August 2015.

Colin, thanks for agreeing to this interview. On your Joong Do Kwan web site (JoongDoKwan.com), you provide some biographical information, and call yourself Chung Sah Nim. You report that you earned your first black belt in "an eclectic Chinese/Korean system out of Southeast Asia" in 1987. Can you tell us more about this system and what region/part of Southeast Asia? What made that system eclectic? How does it differ from and how is it similar to what you teach today? What similarities does it share? What is Joong Do Kwan?

There is sometimes a burning desire to add more to a school in an attempt to do better by your students. It might begin at the start of your journey as you push yourself physically. Then you practice to hone your mind. Then you take on challenges to test yourself. And then years later you might arrive at a syllabus which seems woefully inadequate. A syllabus which does not reflect the quality you've achieved. And your mind goes into overdrive to try and show the world how much better you can make it. Well, I'm over that.

Joong Do Kwan, my school, in fact was named 'The School of the Middle Way' in a bid to remind us that we can tap from the past as much as we can tap from modern innovations. The middle way is also a nice way to reflect the culture of my school, a platform where I am not necessarily top of a hierarchy - merely one of the influences in a student's progress. While we practice in a small garage dojang, we do court a fairly large network of local and international martial artists. I do this because of the organisations I represent, my preserving and promoting the lineage I've inherited, and the obligation I feel to

Colin Wee as a black belt, circa 1987. Can you pick Colin out of the group?

share the best of mudo or budo, the Warrior's path, with everyone.

The adoption of Chung Sah Nim or the 'Chief Instructor' title in my email signature, a Tang Soo Do uniform, and the establishment of Joong Do Kwan's name was to celebrate the Korean heritage of Traditional Taekwondo. The rank stripes, the titles, the patches, are all trappings that were critical insofar as we had to have them in order to leave them behind. Our core practice is and always has been - the struggle between two hara. Hara in Japanese meaning your structural essence or physiological energy. In this understanding of JDK, we definitely see methodological differences in my early training in what I call that 'eclectic system,' to my training in the US in Traditional Taekwondo and Aikido, and to how I unfold skill progression now.

The eclectic system I got my first black belt in is called Ninjado, a truly cringe-worthy name perfect for Singapore in the 1980s. It consisted of Taekwondo kicks, basic Hapkido locks and throws, Chinese patterns, a mixed bag of Chinese/Philippino weapon patterns, and some neigong training. In truth, I'm not totally embarassed - the time spent in Ninjado was appropriate for me, and as I revisit the training with the insight I now have, I am able to benefit from my master's tactical knowledge in ways we hadn't explored back then.

Fast forward only four years to 1991. You joined the American Karate and Taekwondo Organization (AKATO) in Dallas, Texas in the United States. That is a long way from Southeast Asia. What took you to Dallas? The Moo Duk Kwan, I believe, had a large presence in Texas at this time, and still do, if I am not mistaken. Which organizations did you consider, if any, before joining AKATO? What dissuaded you from joining them? What persuaded you to join AKATO?

I went to Dallas for college. If you have to know, I wouldn't have qualified for university in Singapore because I couldn't pass the educational prerequisites for a second language. Simply stating it - I had a really bad attitude towards studying mandarin because of many years of mistreatment and corporal punishment at the hands of a very abusive primary school teacher. I quickly became inured to the punishment, I developed a strength of will but unfortunately also a resistance to studying under him. Eventually you could say there were 'ancillary' benefits as I gravitated towards a contact sport. But no, it wasn't the most positive way to encourage a child.

For your timeline, I started martial arts in 1983, and when I got to Dallas in 1991, had already 8 years of training. There was no real grand plan. I was exercising in the gym early on, saw a flyer that stated there were martial arts classes in American Karate, contacted the teacher in charge, showed him I wasn't a rabble-rouser, and the rest is history. What I loved about SMU Martial Arts Club was the warm welcome I received and the quality and commitment of all their black belts. In addition, I don't want to boast, but they had a policy of black belts train for free. So I plugged into their generosity and started to forge myself into the best practitioner I could be. I did think to look beyond AKaTo, but when you have a line up of a dozen or more multi-style black belts, in regular weekly classes, all of whom have 20 to 30 years or more of practice, how much better could it get?

Both my primary teachers were teaching me their Taekwondo, their Aikido, and their Karate. But they mentored me in other ways, and they have continued to guide me to become a better person over the twenty plus years I've left college. It is unsurprising how much loyalty I feel to them, to Grandmaster Keith Yates, and to AKaTO even now.

Colin, it would certainly seem that you have made the most of your training experiences from the very start. Your early training obviously kept your interest, as you studied it for eight years. What triggered your interest in the martial arts as a boy? What kept

Colin meets up with his "primary teachers" Mr. Proctor and Mr. Robbins whenever he visits Dallas. (Left): Colin is updated on Mr Robbins new syllabus in 2013. (Right): Colin shows Mr Proctor in 2006 that he has Grandmaster Yates forms book on Kindle - an invaluable resource anywhere in the world.

An Interview With Sabumnim Colin Wee

your interest during this period? Is Ninjado pronounced Nin-jahdoe or Ninja-doe (please forgive my poor phonetics!)?

I was a fat kid. I was soft. I was a mummy's boy. Not that any of these are bad in themselves, and certainly nowadays you could thrive regardless of your BMI. But Asia in the late 70s and 80s was an unforgiving place. There were taunts and snide remarks. Exclusion from games. Worse, being the last to be chosen by the team captain, stuck in 'defence,' and then having to be on the side where you had to take your shirt off!

Martial arts, or what was represented on TV as martial arts, was a very welcome outlet. Whether it was the wuxia genre, *Green Hornet*, or *The Man from U.N.C.L.E.*, they were all a departure from a reality where you wore your discipline a few belt notches too wide. I guess you can say I grew tired of being tired. So I eventually started my own portion control diet at the age of 11years old, and loss a significant amount of weight before hitting high school. Then I got offered the opportunity to start martial arts training, took it, and never looked back.

Throughout life, I never had a problem with commitment. The trait had as yet to surface when I was a child, but martial arts brought it out in a big way. I would practice with other martial art students in school, share information about what we've learned in training, and swap martial art books we've purchased. After school I'd be practicing techniques for an hour every day, and then incorporating weight training with the dumbells I had. Not sure I needed to do anything to keep up my interest. I was practising every day and I simply couldn't get enough of it.

Colin, 15, demonstrates some martial artsy stuff in front of his school. Colin admits, "I didn't realise that no one really was that entertained except for the guys who were doing the demo with me."

How is Ninjado pronounced? Are we still dragging that one out? Here's a tip with Asian languages, without knowing accents or the tonal inflection, each word should have equal emphasis. It's dissimilar to English.

How did you decide to make Texas your new home when you came to the U.S.? How did you choose your college? What did you study? Did you complete the requirements for your degree? How has this study affected your martial arts, if at all?

Cox School of business in Dallas, Texas, came highly recommended by my brother-in-law, ticked the right boxes for what I was looking for in a school, and the plus was I had family close by for support and help. I could do a lot of research into other institutions but the reality was I really didn't know what I didn't know. Eventually, Cox

School of Business turned out to be an excellent choice for me on so many levels. Yes, I was hungry to work hard, enjoyed the challenges and eventually completed my basic business degree in Organisation Behaviour with honors, specialising in e-commerce. How did this affect my martial arts, if any? Well, it put me on a path to work with some really interesting online and e-commerce projects that required me to take the lead in situations and teams with very little rules or parameters established. I became very used to getting creative at all levels, from strategisation to operations to information systems. This became the norm for me and by extension influenced the way I saw martial arts. The structure and the rules are always there, but you get used to flying between the spaces and making the entire puzzle work for you rather than against you.

You mentioned "primary teachers" in AKATO earlier in this interview, and how they have continued to mentor you over the past 20+ years. These teachers sound like outstanding role models. You seem to have been fortunate with your relationships with them. I know I, for one, would have appreciated mentors such as these. Who do you consider to be your primary teachers, and how have they continued to mentor and help you mature in the martial arts?

My primary teachers are Mr. Bryan Robbins and Mr. Michael Proctor. Mr. Robbins was my Taekwondo teacher, and Mr. Proctor was my Karate teacher.

I remember the first time back to Dallas in 2006 after many years of not being there – Mr. Robbins held a special class to catch me up on all of the things I'd missed whilst I had been away. Everyone was present, but he was teaching solely for me to understand where he had taken his school. Then in a separate session at Mr. Proctor's class, he walked over to me, concerned that I was wearing an unadorned belt, expressed concern, and asked if anyone was mentoring me whilst I was not in Dallas.

When I return, I feel like I'm coming back to family. Each of them make time to see me socially. Or they'd organise gatherings with other peers and/or with Grandmaster Yates. And they would talk to me about issues that are important to them, important to their practice, and perhaps important to their legacy. Of course, the best thing about being back in Dallas is for me to train with them again and for them to give me feedback. I have of course grown as a martial artist, so the feedback is not because I'm lacking but it informs me of how they are developing as practitioners too.

Some of their progress is conceptual - and I'm able to take that to directly improve tactical skills. Or to make throws and takedowns easier. But over and over, I return to Dallas and find myself respecting and admiring these gentlemen more over the years. The path of budo affects us all, and they have been on it far longer than I have. They make me proud of the training I've received from them. They make me treasure values, the Tenets, and Nijukun. And they remind me how important it is to be grounded in reality.

Take for example taxi rides. Mr. Proctor is not a rich man in a financial sense, but he says taxi drivers should get a good tip because it's hard to make a living driving people around. So now whenever I'm in a Taxi or Uber, I make sure to drop a tip for the driver - and I think about my teacher whenever I do so. It's the little things.

Colin, I know sometimes that students ask questions and seek guidance for which their instructors or teachers do not have answers and/or cannot provide helpful direction or insights. I suspect this has happened to you. Can you recall an instance in your personal experience after asking for direction or insight? Can you describe the

experience? How did you proceed or progress after the event? Have you been on the receiving end as a student asked you a question for which you did not have a ready answer? How did you proceed or approach that instance?

The questions I ask myself these days focus on trying to understand the expert behind the patterns, as opposed to trying to decipher the patterns. Sometimes some things just come together and hey presto, an application coalesces to match the technique sequence. More often than not however, it takes insight upon insight, constant exploration, and non-stop testing to ensure that the concepts fit AND work for us. In this way we are asking many many questions, most of which don't get readily answered. And when we do happen on the answer from either our research, or working with other instructors, we can then use this knowledge to retrospectively look at all those earlier questions.

As for being an all-knowledgeable resource ... well, we can only teach to the best of our abilities.

Many know of Grandmaster Keith Yates through his books. Many, however, may not be familiar with Grandmaster Yates. Do you recall your first meeting with Grandmaster Yates? How would you describe your experiences with him? Which of his books do you feel are his best, and how might those books benefit the average student of Taekwondo?

Grandmaster Yates came to my weekly practice sessions maybe once or twice during the years I was in Dallas. While I of course saw him several times at other events, that first time he led class, he mentioned how much he liked the way I formed my knife hand block. Essentially turning the blade of the hand out so that that would be the first thing that connects with the opponent.

Colin receives A-KaTo Instructor of the Year in 2016. He had been invited back for their 40th Anniversary Celebration in March, held in Dallas. The highly unexpected award for Instructor of the Year was an emotional moment for Colin in his 33+ year martial art career. "Grandmaster Keith Yates is one of the most inspiring gentlemen I know," Colin notes.

The professional relationship we have developed over the last decade however, has taken my understanding of the man to a new level. He has been supportive of my training, my research, and the resource videos I share online. Socially when we meet, he has been inclusive and has welcomed me as a senior practitioner - in fact making me feel welcomed as member of his martial family.

As you have intimated, Grandmaster Yates has an extensive line of books he has authored. Of the several I own, I might say 'American Karate and Tae Kwon Do' might be a good one to own. It's basically an intro book that covers general topics of interest to a beginner in the martial arts. However, Grandmaster Yates does address issues which help you understand his values like Martial Arts and Religion, '"Master" Rankings and Titles," and differences between 'American' and 'Olympic' Tae Kwon Do.

And by 'values,' this would be what is the most defining attribute of Grandmaster Yates and AKaTo. Once a few years ago, I came into contact with an international certificate mill, and was gobsmacked by the promotions, certificates, the fancy titling, the flashy red belts, and martial art resumes of practitioners younger than me threatening to exceed an A4 sheet of paper. When I go back to Dallas, I see none of this. Most of Grandmaster Yates' black belts train non-commercially in halls, at their local 'Y', with small groups of students, and have been doing so for absolute years. When I return, my teachers want to catch me up on the things I've missed, talk to me of their martial family, and they want to see pictures of my children. Because I'm not familiar with the parking anymore, I've had a fist full of dollars shoved in my hand so I can pay for parking. Because I come back so infrequently, I've had autographed books, magazines, and DVDs gifted to me. Because I tell them my muscles ache as I've gotten older, they sponsor me to come with them to their yoga session.

I am not sure I can praise Grandmaster Yates - nor the people he has chosen to surround himself with, enough.

Grandmaster Keith Yates has trained with martial arts legends Skipper Mullins and Jhoon Rhee, and has been photographed with many of them, as well as martial arts blood-and-guts legend Allen Steen, founder of AKATO, as well. Have you likewise met such legends as a member of AKATO and/or trained with them? Can you tell us about your experiences when you met them?

At the AKaTo Banquet in 2016, these luminaries (except for GM Jhoon Rhee) were sitting at Table 1, and I was placed on Table 2. I think GM Allen Steen did share a few words but whatever he did say, he is ultimately my grandmaster's senior. All of them are. And therefore, until I get the opportunity to know them better, I view them through a lens influenced by how I view Grandmaster Yates. As for training with them, I don't feel I particularly need to. I've got my own teachers. And, might I say, my teachers are doing a fairly good job.

You call your Taekwondo "traditional." Traditional is a difficult definition in most circles, yet you explicitly choose to use it to describe the art that you practice. You also list that one of your teachers taught Karate. What are the differences, in your opinion, between Karate and Taekwondo in general? What in your experience defines "traditional Taekwondo" as you describe your art? Why do you call your art Taekwondo, not Karate?

My lineage was brought out of Korea in the 1950s by GM Jhoon Rhee, settled in the Southwest USA, and was practiced in close proximity to its Karate brothers way before the ITF and WTF were formed. When I happened on it, it was mostly called American Karate, but the term Traditional Taekwondo is fairly accurate given the forms as we have received them have not really changed much since. I continue the practice of the forms I've learned, but I do run a rather progressive little dojang. This means I am pushing the boundaries of skills and applications of my

An Interview With Sabumnim Colin Wee

system. I do so by applying skills I've learned, research into precursors of my martial system, cross training with other martial stylists, and continually testing the technique sequences of our patterns. Tradition to me is not some dusty form in need of a revamp - it is a living breathing system that adapts to the environment at large.

What is the difference between Taekwondo and Karate? Which Karate? Whose Karate? And what Taekwondo are you talking about? You talking about a little Samurai program? If so, it's just some labelling on a certificate or differences in marketing slogans. If you want to talk in general terms, most Taekwondo schools preference kicks over punches. For Sport or Shotokan Karate, they gravitate towards a stylistic kumite which requires them to display their 'pull back hand', or their stances, or identifiable fundamental strikes.

In my school, Taekwondo to me is a hard style program that communicates martial content using basic techniques, patterns and free sparring. At higher levels, the patterns create opportunities to drill students in fundamental combative skills. As hard styles go, much of this is a prescriptive approach to dynamic situations. We engage an opponent and funnel this attrition towards a handful of solutions that we have drilled over and over again.

When this approach faces off a modern Taekwondo practitioner, we often see an opponent preferring to engage at the mid to long range kicking distances. Exploratory kicks would come from snappy roundhouse kicks to the outside of the body, whilst front kicks or side kicks attempt to reach the core. And then there are those sneaky hook kicks that go head high or the inside S kicks which go between the guard.

Of the Karate guys we've faced, most of them use the thigh kick similar to Muay Thai fighters to chop at our base. And then strong body punches, jabs to head or spinning back fists to head. Those who do Shotokan and variants also go for the mid range reverse snap punch - which are deceptive as they do generate a good body blow.

When Colin returned for the 40th anniversary of AkaTo in 2016, he participated in a closed door training session for out-of-towners, led by Grandmaster Keith Yates and Colin's Instructor, Sensei Mike Proctor. "I think this session we were playing around with gap closing skills, and perhaps an irimi and eventual takedown that draws the head backward and then toward the floor," Colin notes. It was all smiles in this photo, but before - I made sure to apply a huge amount of pain onto this young man, from the grabbing of skinfold, applying pressure onto his neck, finger strikes, and then immobilising him on the floor. I wanted to share my 'traditional' take on the skills he was already practicing. And then I insisted that he apply it back on me. I was very impressed with his attitude, his enthusiasm, and his ability."

I think the more these other practitioners engage in their style-only type competitions, the less fun it is fighting as they become stylistically predictable. This is in no way disrespecting their art or their effort in any way. Nor their abilities. I just feel the more restrictive the style is, the less growth a practitioner enjoys in later years.

Why do I call my art Taekwondo? There is cultural significance to the progress our system made from China, to Japan, to Korea, and then the US. Not to call it Taekwondo would be telling an incomplete story. Identifying it as a Korean art does not detract from its predecessors nor all that its source material can be. And it is just right I acknowledge and honour the difficulties and challenges the Korean people have experienced throughout history.

In a recent interview, you describe your training at AKATO among a variety of martial arts and artists. One specific experience you share deals with crossing the distance to an opponent. Your describe that your instructor magically closed this distance for a punch more suited for a mid to long range kick, but you were never instructed how to perform that closing technique. So you went home one day, went to your backyard, and worked at doing the same until you figured out how to generate the acceleration, how to employ the proper body dynamics. You say that the technique was so good that you had to refrain from using it because it couldn't be stopped. Which instructor so inspired you? Can you describe and instruct us on this technique here so that we may work on it as well? Would you describe this technique as traditional?

That was a distinct event and a powerful memory just because it shook me up. Here I thought it was all about snappy kicks and kodak moments, and when I brought that up against a true master, things just didn't go the way I thought they would. I didn't know that practitioner very well that first time, but in subsequent years he became one of my main instructors, and gave me the strength so I can wear my black belt proudly. As our relationship has evolved he has also started sharing more of his values and ideals. This I think is as valuable as the tactics I've learned from him.

As for this particular technique - it's simply a lunging punch. But rather than taking a step like you were walking, you drive the move like you were making one sprint at a time. This for me was how I immediately understood where my mistake was - that the analogy I used of 'stepping', essentially picking up your leg and swinging it forward was incorrect. It seems like the same motion, but once you change that one little mental instruction, the tactic gains combative value.

Would this technique be traditional? Very much so. :-)

In that same interview, you indicate that you initially thought patterns practice was ridiculous, yet the other AKATO black belts outmaneuvered you, despite your peak physical condition (having just exited the Army prior to moving to the States). So you plunged yourself into the practice of patterns. Can you tell us about that experience of focusing on patterns, which patterns, and the benefits you derived from them? How has your approach or use of patterns changed over time? What do you therefore teach today concerning patterns?

I was a first degree belt belt, with a mind fixated on power, speed and flexibility. That's all that I knew because had been my entire diet up to that point. Like Icarus, I was self-absorbed and arrogant. Then I came into contact with the black belts at AKaTo. That was an early eye opening moment and got me thinking that I had to change my approach to the martial arts. Maybe I was wrong? Maybe I'm lacking something? Maybe I'm not training correctly? I promptly decided I should give their way a go. So, yeah, I ignored my initial dismissal of traditional forms and plunged into learning them like they did. Which patterns? I learned them all! While the sequences were very different, I learned them quickly. Understanding the traditional forms, however, took longer than I expected.

How has my approach to patterns changed over time? Simply this - the pattern doesn't teach you. The pattern is an opportunity for your teacher to transmit knowledge gained from experience. Forms are also a tool for your personal skill set. For many years I thought patterns were the be all and end all of martial arts. That is not true. Patterns are only a syllabus. What you do with them as an instructor determines how much you and your students grow. If you rely on pure repetition of forms, you're going to be an extremely limited instructor, and practitioner. Instead, seek to understand what the expert who created the forms wished to remember and transmit to those who practice them.

Do you feel the Ch'ang Hon patterns are derived from Karate patterns or do they contain other elements, techniques, surprises or wisdom?

I understand what you're asking, and the most straightforward answer I can offer is - the Ch'ang Hon patterns might as well be Shotokan Karate patterns.

Colin attended AKaTo's 40th Anniversary Banquet Dinner, 2016, where he was named Instructor of the Year. From left, Colin's old training partner, Jon Alster; Colin's instructor Mr. Bryan Robbins; another old sparring buddy Tim Pugliese, and Colin himself. Colin led a training session during the 40th Anniversary celebration, and Mr. Robbins was really interested to know how the session went. Colin told him, "I bombed out spectacularly, but that's alright because I put the blame totally on you." Fortunately, Colin also gave Mr. Robbins a bottle of booze so that he could enjoy a few drinks while wondering exactly how badly Colin had represented him.

Of course however, simple answers don't do a great job unfolding a good story. Chang Hon patterns aren't Karate patterns because they were created by Korean practitioners and their lineage is straight from the heart of Korean culture. They may have once been derivative of Shotokan, but I've never thought that practising them would lock me into a Shotokan methodology. In fact, knowing there's a linking allowed me to see past Japanese Karate to its inevitable ties to Okinawan Karate, and Chinese Wushu.

In the previous question you asked how I now use the patterns. In this question you want to know if the patterns contain additional surprises. Here's a glimpse of a progression of my thinking from just last month - which I declared 'Yulgok' month. Meaning, we would go through Yulgok and train its applications through the course of the entire month. Before we started, I went through the videos from the last 2 years, and I decided to focus on several applications for our senior belts. During the session, I would share and we would practice applications from the pattern. During our practice, I would fine tune the applications or finesse our skills, and then link what we were doing to other applications from other patterns. And every now and then I would apply the technique differently to stretch the student into understanding various tactics befitting the situation they are in. When I say I would stretch the technique - most of the time I might never have used the technique in that particular way before. I apply the technique based on martial concepts, my experience, and the goals at hand. In that way, yes, I would say the patterns come up with surprises all the time.

In the recent interview mentioned above, you provide a list of folks who have inspired you over the years, I presume. Can you select a few of these influences and describe what you have been able to learn from them. Those listed include Iain Abernathy, Stuart Anslow, Bruce Clayton, Dan Djurdjevic, Onaga Yoshimitsu, Taira Masaji, Tony Tan Suan Hee, Motobu Choki, Michael Proctor, Bryan Robbins, Tim White, Kelly Worden and Keith Yates.

It's easy to look at an industry expert and say how great he looks. How slick is his production. How lovely is his tatami.

Can I speak to you of other folks who have inspired me to become better as an instructor? Who are they? My students. Not just the brightest or most talented - but all of them. My students are the driving force in me asking - how do I make them tougher opponents? How do I solve the problem of performing under fight and flight conditions? How do take the least number of techniques to create the most amount of utility? How do I make them understand combative concepts? What techniques do they naturally gravitate to - and why?

Looking at an expert and following him is easy. For me I could probably mimic a good amount of stuff anyone shows me. But to make a skill my own, I need it to fit within the paradigm of our system. If it doesn't fit, its value diminishes greatly. It's not like there's no value ... it's just that it doesn't make the whole bigger than the sum of its parts.

You have had an interesting point of view on many topics which differ from common public opinion. I appreciate that you have often revealed a two-dimensional idea to be exactly that, flat and narrow. For example, I say that your viewpoint is a little left of center. When one stands in a different place, however – such as left of center – and looks back to center, the perspective, scenery and relationships – and thus our understanding of the original topic – magically change forever. I appreciated your article in the October 2017 issue of *Totally Tae Kwon Do*, in which you

discuss that martial arts teaches techniques, some obviously lethal, without considering the legal and moral responsibilities due to the nature of training and common safety equipment. Is that a fair summarization?

Ironically my first thought is to digress from the question ...

Often, a person's worldview is influenced by early or powerful life experiences. My worldview owes a lot to the generosity, the welcome, and the nurturing I encountered when I trained with AKATO. My story seems polar opposite to the many instances of unfavourable experiences so prevalent in this industry. There, I found myself week-to-week standing amongst a dozen or more black belts from various styles. And there we all practised hard but maintained a collegiate, respectful, and congenial training environment.

So while I seem to differ from "common public opinion," I'm no rebel. I don't have a chip on my shoulder. And I've been around the block enough to be real, knowing what I'm good at and what I need work on. What has occurred to me is that I have a gift of being able to see a situation, and then to simply state what I believe to be true.

In that article for Totally Tae Kwon Do I wanted to talk holistically about self-control, the difficulty of self defence, and appropriate use of force. We cannot fake ourselves to think we can "practice lethal martial arts with impunity." We shouldn't dismiss this discussion with simple one liners like "better to be judged by 12 than carried by 6." And we owe it to our students to have self defence tactics that are both morally and legally sound.

Colin, I am glad that your experience with AKATO was a great influence in your martial career. As you note, it is counter to the experience of many others who try to train with martial artists from other disciplines, including my own. I am

Niaal Holder, Colin's student, faces a narrow corridor of opponents determined to not let him pass during an unconventional but symbolic black belt testing. "The way in martial arts is often analogous to these physical analogies," Colin Wee writes. In this case, Niaal must overcome an impossible challenge, and going beyond it allows the individual to reflect on this success. He could of course choose not to do it. At which time the grading would be cancelled, he would most likely quit the school, and discover that no one really cares. Of course the instructor bears each student's burden in his own way. But after all, this journey is a personal one - and you can choose to see the positive or you can dwell on the negative. It is up to you. Like other events on the path, it's hard to really capture the essence of what an individual takes away on their own subjective journey."

curious how that actually worked at AKATO with so many black belts from several disciplines. Can you explain how and why these black belt classes were successful? For example, how were classes organized? What was the curriculum? Did everyone practice the same things during these black belt classes although they were from various arts? How might one duplicate this experience?

I don't want to over-generalise, but many of the instructors at AKaTo train small groups out of hired premises. Most are traditional martial artists who naturally respect the ranking system, but then they also have high dan-level members who are worthy of respect. Another great equaliser I find is that everyone spars each other - hard and often. This kind of shared intensity bonds people together in ways other organisations can't do. Where I trained, it was called the SMU Martial Arts Club, with a primary syllabus consisting of Chang Hon forms. However, since there were many other stylists there, as we broke up to work on our own forms, they would do the same but on their forms. Might not have been the most efficient or the most tightly orchestrated of groups, but it seemed to work and the sharing of skills helped everyone grow.

You are involved with IAOMAS (International Alliance of Martial Arts Schools). Please tell us about IAOMAS. How did it get its start? What is your history with the organization? What is your current role with IAOMAS?

In the early days of my starting my school here in Perth, I started to reach out to other instructors on the internet to understand their research and their approach to martial arts. I was working on my own syllabus, and had many loose ends that needed tying together. I am not entirely sure how it happened but I met Stuart Anslow, now one of my good friends and who's a fairly well-known Taekwondo author and personality. Stuart was talking to me of IAOMAS and his idea of networking amongst martial artists. Frankly, I couldn't see the logic. Why on earth would I want to expose myself to egomaniacs, McDojo owners, and other toxic martial art types? But fortunately for me, I tried to keep an open mind, and after Stuart showed me one of the earlier events he had organised, I tried to do the same here in Perth. As it happened, the end of 2003 found me in the UK, and training with Stuart's renowned Rayners Lane Taekwon-do Academy. When I say 'training with,' in reality Stuart asked me to lead his class. Or should I say Stuart Anslow - a highly respected instructor - allowed a total stranger from the opposite side of the world to lead a training session on his behalf. This was a huge lesson in trust, and I am happy to say I have learned many more lessons from Stuart and from his vision of IAOMAS. This was how I started with IAOMAS, simply beginning with

Colin with Stuart Anslow and two of his black belts at Rayners Lane Taekwon-do Academy, in the UK, in 2003

An early IAOMAS event in October 2004 where Colin invited Debbie Clarke from Southern Cross Bujutsu to his school - during a time when he had loads of newbies. Colin invited Debbie so she could promote her involvement with the Women in Martial Arts group. Colin laments that Facebook at that time was not the giant it is today or they would have been able to jointly market it more successfully.

an understanding of what friendship meant in the martial arts.

IAOMAS started with three practitioners - Stuart Anslow in the UK, Dave Melton in the US, and Tim Posynick in Canada. There was a huge uptake in those early days - people were coming on board, sticking the IAOMAS logo on their websites, and we had volunteers create and manage HTML web pages with lists and lists of martial art schools. In the first one or two years we had 600 over schools worldwide. From the excitement came cross training events between different schools, and a huge amount of interaction on the IAOMAS forum. Mostly however, I'd say instructors would benefit from the IAOMAS concept. We would seek out other instructors we'd have communicated with online. We might hang out for coffees and beers, or even train when we travel to new schools. Few students however took up the privilege of IAOMAS concept of two weeks of free training for travelling students.

Several years after, with the activity on the forum mostly killed by social media, I volunteered to take stewardship of IAOMAS. Honestly speaking, I did let the ball drop several times over the last decade. In 2013 however, I reconceptualised IAOMAS as a networking organisation and organised the first ever IAOMAS Martial Arts Conference for 2014 here in Perth. During the ramp up phase, I hosted and facilitated many joint training events between the schools, and continued to drum up networking online. It was slightly different orchestrating it with a more regional presence - I discovered I had to deal with many more interpersonal agendas, and politics than if I were organising a pure online event. However, I persevered, and I believed I've done a really good job developing a strong network for myself and IAOMAS here in Western Australia.

My current role in IAOMAS? I am trying to hand over the reigns of Coordinator to another person who is interested to lead the expansion of IAOMAS. I would have liked for this role to have gone to another country and for myself to be retained as a behind-the-scenes Chairman so there's always someone there to steer the ship. But ... like anything, it's hard to get the right volunteer.

Colin, if I am not mistaken, I believe you have hosted several professional development seminars in Perth, Australia. Can you explain how these came about, what they are, how they relate to IAOMAS and its members, and the impact they have had for IAOMAS, attendees, & etc.?

I am an instructor who has 4-6 students and who trains in a garage. And my secret skill is to extend my hand in friendship, to draw a network of diverse instructors together, and to help them enjoy the benefits of all of our expertise. Last year, I thought that instead of another IAOMAS conference, I would organise a Continuing Professional Development series for high level instructors here in Perth. I would host them from my garage, to keep numbers low and the setting intimate, I would get a few of them to volunteer as instructors, and I would organise lunch afterward. It has quickly become one of the best training events in Perth. Can you imagine a dozen heads of schools coming together and training? Even if they weren't instructing, just having any one of them as your training partner would be an amazing opportunity. So yeah, they come from far and wide, to share amongst themselves. They can talk about anything they care about - it doesn't even need to be a physical lesson. One of the modules from the last session we had saw Terence Bridgeman, a Savate veteran, roll out his collection of daggers. He talked about their history and their make, and then led us through European knife sparring concepts. How amazing is that breadth of exposure? I'm still blown away. And I organise this!

Colin in mid-takedown with Damien Merrin, a really nice, independent, and fairly successful Taekwondo instructor at a joint seminar with Taekwondo Kidokwan in April 2017. Colin's early aiki training is clearly evident (notice the finger pointing downward). Colin's bottom hand, however, shows the departure from where he started, and Mr. Merrin's head position also shows tactical development from hard style training.

What does it mean to become a member of IAOMAS?

It takes a great deal of courage for school owners to get out of their comfort zone, believe in an external organisation, and to take initiative in contacting us. I hope they see from our social media presence, the website, and the interactions online that we are social networking group first and foremost, and

An Interview With Sabumnim Colin Wee

Colin leads a freebie seminar in Perth titled "Smash with Your Foot" in February 2012.

that we have no intention of applying top down controls of any kind on their school, their method of teaching, or any part of their operations.

Next, while we always send out an open invitation, we are very careful who we let into the organisation. Frankly, I'd not have IAOMAS become a certificate mill nor would I want those species of martial artists who subscribe to certificate mills on board our group. If you come to us with a resume the length of my arm, are too young for all those accolades, there is a high chance we will push back on admission. If on the other hand, you are sincerely looking forward to networking with our group, have an open mind and an open door policy - we will warmly welcome you to our group, will help you promote yourself on social media, support student training and incentivisation initiatives, and link you with other practitioners who have the same interests as you.

The big thing I think about IAOMAS is that the organisation is about 'values' leadership. We care about solid individuals who will benefit from networking with other solid individuals. We believe that courtesy, humility, friendship, and caring are great traits that will help you and your students grow. I myself see it in others who are linked with me, but my personal experience provides enough of a compelling belief that every new person you meet on your path can help you improve some aspect of yourself. If only you are open to the experience and from learning from it.

Let's pretend I am a school owner and member of IAOMAS. How can I best leverage that membership? How might I use my association with IAOMAS to network with other instructors in my region? Where might someone like this start and move forward?

In the early days of IAOMAS, I was told by Stuart just go meet up with new schools, tell them what IAOMAS is all about, and maybe invite them to a joint training or group conference. It does take some getting used to - trying to get up the courage, then make your pitch, expect to be rejected (or not), and then expend more effort organising what needs to be a fun and casual event where you give it your all so people get to know you. This approach works but it only works because potential (and real) members of IAOMAS have an open heart, and are ready to give you the benefit of the doubt. It doesn't do anything to allay their misgivings about your agenda nor help stop them being wary that you're going to steal their students or denounce their style.

Nowadays, I take a much cooler approach to IAOMAS. And perhaps I can do that because I am one of the more connected instructors here in Western Australia. So here's what I do - I don't try to do anything much. I'm just myself, and I just try to meet up with new people and make new friends. If they practice martial arts, that's a plus - and I'll share with them what IAOMAS is, and what we do. And if they look like they're not absolute idiots and might make a good potential member, I invite them along. I also then extend myself to help them market themselves, network with other people, and promote the activities they're doing. In short I am ready to help them with their own organisational needs, as I can.

Every now and then I put on my uniform and also show them that I can play nice with others. That even if I stand for values and Tenets, I am not too full of myself. And I will give people the benefit of the doubt.

I have not met you in person, correct? But you carry yourself well online, and on the videos I have seen. I anticipate when I meet you in real life, I'm going to like you as much as I do over FaceBook or email. That's all we need, really. For you to just extend yourself. If anything was the secret of IAOMAS, this would be it.

In regular events, IAOMAS seminars would

Guest instructor Colin Wee teaches a takedown and follow up elbow lock or strike at Kidokwan Perth with a fellow black belt.

Colin launched the IAOMAS Masters Event at our second continuing professional development session in July 2017. Nenad leads this particular slot, and in the background is Debbie Clarke (wearing glasses - whom Colin first invited to my dojang in 2004). On her right is Master Robert Ho, who brought Taekwondo to Western Australia, and on her left is Senior Master Peter Wong who leads Taekwondo Kidokwan (with whom Colin is affiliated). Sifu Gawain Siu in the red jacked founded Free Form Fighting, an amateur full contact event, which Colin judges.

be held in someone's training hall, and will involve no fees except maybe a 'gold coin' donation. 'Gold coin' donation meaning a small token sum to cover rent. It may feature three guest instructors in half a morning, who lead a 40 minute session for all other stylists who participate. I try to coordinate events using a theme or some logical sequence but it isn't necessary. Make sure the organiser welcomes and thanks everyone whilst sharing the goals of the event and the importance of sharing. Get a group photo and post some feel good message on FaceBook. It's that simple.

IAOMAS, however, is not in the business of conferences or seminars. It is as much a coffee or whisky event sitting down with another person who is as passionate as you, and who is looking for like-minded practitioners. In this world of MMA, of egos, and of being assailed by a barrage of marketing nonsense, people want to find those individuals who like you, or like me, have dedicated themselves to their art, and who are looking to just enjoy the company of others who do the same.

You make it sound so easy, Colin! I can appreciate that there is a measure of courage required to meet new people, especially when they are likely to ask themselves what you are selling and are certain they won't and don't want it. What are your plans for IAOMAS for the near future? Can any of the members propose ideas for the organization?

I guess some skill at selling an idea may work in your favour. But given I'm not really selling anything for money, it's not sales nor am I a salesman in the classic sense. If

Colin and Stuart (Anslow) always have fun when they meet up! Here they recreate a well known photo of General Choi and Kim Jong-II

I feel resistance and a misalignment from whomever I'm meeting, I am happy just to talk about the organisation in general terms and let the invite pass. Literally I chose not to close those who aren't the right fit for IAOMAS. If they respond to what you are sharing, then go ahead and invite them along, or work out something that is mutually beneficial.

A recent IAOMAS session? Last year, I launched the IAOMAS Master's event - something I felt was needed for continuing professional development amongst senior instructors. Three would volunteer and lead a joint training class, and participants get the chance to practice with high-level, open style instructors.in a collegiate and intimate setting. How did I pull it together? I simply sent an email telling everyone about it, requested for some volunteers, they all showed up, enjoyed the session, and devoured the lunch that I provided.
Frankly, you can't pay for this kind of event. The informality itself puts people at ease, and the discussion amongst peers is at a level that is rarely seen on instructional DVDs or YouTube or even at most commercial training events. And it was held in my little garage.

Obviously, not everyone will be receptive to IAOMAS as you have noted. Generally, how do such initial meetings go? Can you describe their responses, your response to theirs, etc.? Do you have any advice to circumvent their ego?

My guess is that the two main types of instructors who don't want any part of IAOMAS - those who have ego problems and those who are making some money through their practice. Those with ego problems are more or less easy to spot, and it's relatively easy for me not to invite them to future events. Those who are trying to make money may not like it that they need to open their doors to cross training events or travelling guests. Or perhaps the transparency which happens

An Interview With Sabumnim Colin Wee

when other high level instructors visit.

Do I have a way to circumvent ego? No. But I do have some advice for those who are trying to deal nonsense in the world of martial arts.

People get bent out of shape with 9 year old black belts, or XMA pattern competitions, or whatever strip mall marketing that they feel diminishes their own practice. For me, what I do is what I do. If someone thinks what I do is akin to what their child does, so be it. Lots of people see things superficially, and will never understand the depth of my practice until they walk the same path as I have - which is highly unlikely. So what they think will not keep me from the path. I will share the best of my practice with whomever has an open heart and whomever wants to taste from the same fountain of knowledge I drink from.

I understand that you have several international leaders in IAOMAS. Is there a list available on the Internet? What is the best procedure for instructors to join IAOMAS? What are the organization's expectations of members? Can members propose ideas for the organization?

Evidence of Colin's unconventional but effective viewpoint: Hook kick to the groin at Kidokwan Perth in 2014.

Colin poses with Ron Jenson, fellow member of the private Study of Taekwondo Facebook Group, who flew to Dallas to be his demo partner in 2016.

We have very credible people in the organisation, but we aren't using their credentials to sell the network. In the early days one of the mandates was to ensure very little self-aggrandisement occurred through our activities. It was such a priority that I had to push really hard to use the 'Coordinator' title when I needed to administer to this group. I guess if a new instructor or member comes walking in, is invited to sit down with a small and casual group, then discovers that our members do indeed carry some clout, this might go much further than if you see a bunch of young guns with resumes as long as your arm fronting a website for super senior practitioners.

Instructors interested in IAOMAS can log onto FaceBook and search for IAOMAS Free for All - and start a conversation with any one of us. There's no point joining if you don't get to know who's involved, or what we do, or anything about the network. In the end, membership is what you make of it. In other words, how much you get out of it is how much you put into it. Like anything else.

I generally run most of my organisations like democracies until I need to get something done. So if someone wants to step up, do it right, and get something done, I'd love that and would welcome them with open arms. Constructive criticism is welcomed too. But if someone just wants to put in their two cents, or throw an idea into the fray, or push their own agenda - I'll take it on board ... up to a point. In a volunteer organisation my focus has to be extremely clear, and I've got to be as efficient as possible or nothing gets done. But yeah, propose all you want. I'm all ears!

Colin, until recently, I did not know that your father was the Father of Archery in Singapore. I have tried to find more information about him online, but it seems very scarce, although he founded Bill Wee Agencies in 1965. Could you share more about him for readers? Do you feel your father has influenced your martial arts in any way? If so, how?

I started martial arts at 13 years old, but a lifetime before that I was an archer with the Archery Club of Singapore. My father was an avid archer, and as club President, President of the Association, National Champion, and National Team Coach he spent many many hours at the archery ground. I was not as committed, but there's only so much distraction an open field can afford til you return to that bow and fire it a few more times. Eventually, I would have fired many more arrows than the other adults, and that would eventually find me

A very young Colin Wee with his father, Bill Wee.

Colin (center) competes at one of his first archery competitions at Gloucester Barracks in Singapore, 1983.

becoming the youngest archer to have qualified and to represent Singapore on the National Team.

As a competitor, my dad was one of the most consistent and mentally resilient archers. He practiced intelligently, with dedication, and brought this winning mindset to many competitions, dominating the local scene for absolute years. As the President of the club and association, he led with authority and with passion, and earned the respect of both local archers and international players. As National Coach, and as my coach, he was a force to be reckoned with; he was clear on what he wanted to see from his archers (dedication and clean form), he was clear about what he didn't like (smoking and poor equipment), and he had simple maxims that helped archers understand his philosophy when shooting. As a young coach, I didn't always agree with what he said, however, on principle I would always follow to the best of my ability and would never contradict what he said.

Maybe it was that I started archery early, or that I grew up during what many archers nowadays called 'The Golden Era' of archery in Singapore, but I found that I had a highly developed intuitive coaching ability. I could look at physical phenomena, 'see' what was happening using my own kinesthetic understanding, interpret those signals, and then offer explanation and solutions to the archer. I got so good at this that there were times I swear I was plugged into the thought processes archers experienced as they stood in front of me.

As a father, I'm not sure my dad always understood me. But I would be remiss if I didn't say that he was generous with me, many times gave me the benefit of the doubt, and despite being an authoritarian, he was always just an advocate of hard work and dedication - everything I myself now respect and admire. Eventually I think he grew to understand me and my situation - much more than I had given him credit for earlier, and I really appreciated his patience and tolerance - in fact, his entire demeanour - in later years.

Everything I learned in archery, and I also hope my father's blessing, continues to accompany me as a martial artist.

Additional Praise for Colin Wee's *Breaking Through: The Secrets of Bassai Dai Kata*

Breaking Through: The Secrets of Bassai Dai Kata is jammed-packed with essential tactical applications, biomechanical principles, and probing self-study questions that will not only assist you with this particular *kata* but also help facilitate your own martial arts practice. I have been aware of Master Wee's work for years, and I support his continued evolution in the martial arts. This book is filled with golden nuggets of coaching and not only deep dives into the *Bassai Dai* form but also provides you with universal tactical strategies, self-defense scenarios and solutions, coupled with amazing point of view pictures. I highly recommend you add this book to your martial library—I did!

> **Chris Hanson**
> Martial Arts Coach
> Founder of Karate Unity
> @karateunity (YouTube, Facebook, Instagram)
> KarateUnity.ca

As a martial artist of more than 40 years of experience, with roots in three styles of Karate and 30 of those years spent teaching Taekwon-do, I am excited to see that this book takes to heart the "do," or way, of Karate and Taekwon-do. In *Breaking Through: The Secrets of Bassai Dai Kata*, Colin is a not just a martial instructor but a teacher in every sense of the word. In these pages, he at once exercises and demonstrates the "do" of the path he has chosen to best teach martial arts. Colin in this case uses *Bassai*, a common pattern in Karate and Taekwondo, to teach advanced combat skills which all students of the martial arts will find not only interesting and insightful but useful as well.

> **Master John McNally, 7th Dan, Ch'ang Hon Taekwon-do**
> Founder & Chairman, International Taekwondo Council
> Founder & Chairman, Absolute Taekwondo Association (UK)
> International-Taekwondo-Council.com, TKDC.co.uk

Breaking Through is a martial parable of sorts. On one hand, it is the story of Colin Wee's journey, from Singapore to Texas to Australia to the establishment of the *Joong Do Kwan*. On the other hand, Wee takes the traditional practice of patterns found in the striking arts— such as Karate and Taekwondo to name only two— and repurposes them, not as extrinsic solo exercises but as intrinsic components in the study of combat. He demonstrates the process with *Bassai Dai*, a *kata* which has inspired him for decades, extracting twelve lessons—Wee calls them applications—he has unearthed from his study of the pattern. Each application is inspired by sequences of movements found within the *kata*. While others often try to force applications to fit the form, the lessons in *Breaking Through* grow organically from Wee's close and thorough study, an analysis which includes its creator, its history, its intended purpose, the socio political conditions in which it was developed, and an unprejudiced exploration of its techniques against an opponent. Wee's method, which he has dubbed the JDK Method, can be applied to any form, no matter the style. Every martial artist who practices forms, whether novice or expert, can benefit from training and studying Master Wee's applications in *Breaking Through*, before applying the same process to other patterns in their arsenal to discover secrets hidden within them.

Grandmaster Mike Swope, 8th Dan, Chun Kuhn Taekwondo
General Secretary, World Chun Kuhn Taekwondo Federation
Editor/Designer/Publisher at Moosul Publishing, LLC
WorldChunKuhnTKD.com, MoosulPublishing.com

I was always impressed by Colin's take on training forms on his well established YouTube channel. His idea of using the biomechanics of specific techniques and sequences in *kata/hyung/tul* shows an insightful understanding of the martial arts. Today many practitioners unfortunately stick to a sole "what you see is what you get" interpretation of forms. Colin's approach, however, uses underlying principles of movement to offer an endless number of possibilities for useful applications. I would even say this brings back the "martial" to the "art." The quality of the book is outstanding and one can easily spot the love and detail that went into the process of creation. Colin does not limit this masterpiece by showing just technical skills, though. He peppers the book with history and philosophical remarks which help readers understand his unusual training methods regarding *kata*, *Bassai Dai* in this instance. Even without Karate training, one can easily follow along with clear but highly-detailed explanations in text and pictures. Congratulations to Colin for this eye-opening book!

Master Claus Moos, 5th Degree, Jae-Hwa Kwon Style Taekwondo
Head Instructor at KWON Martial Arts Center, Ingolstadt/ Donau (Germany)
Kwon-In.de

www.ingramcontent.com/pod-product-compliance
Lightning Source LLC
Chambersburg PA
CBHW041230020526
44118CB00046B/2848